# Exploring Practices of Ministry

FOUNDATIONS FOR LEARNING

EXPLORING
# PRACTICES OF MINISTRY
PAMELA COOPER-WHITE
MICHAEL COOPER-WHITE

EXPLORING PRACTICES OF MINISTRY

Copyright © 2014 Fortress Press. All rights reserved. Except for brief quotations in critical articles or reviews, no part of this book may be reproduced in any manner without prior written permission from the publisher. Visit http://www.augsburgfortress.org/copyrights/ or write to Permissions, Augsburg Fortress, Box 1209, Minneapolis, MN 55440.

Cover design: Laurie Ingram
Book design: PerfecType, Nashville, TN

*Library of Congress Cataloging-in-Publication Data is available*
Print ISBN: 978-1-4514-8893-7
eBook ISBN: 978-1-4514-8973-6

The paper used in this publication meets the minimum requirements of American National Standard for Information Sciences — Permanence of Paper for Printed Library Materials, ANSI Z329.48-1984.

Manufactured in the U.S.A.

We dedicate this book to all our students, past, present, and future, who are also our teachers in the shared practices of ministry.

# Contents

# Figures

# Acknowledgments

For this book on the practices of ministry, we are indebted to the countless practitioner colleagues whose ministries over the past decades have inspired and informed our own. In dozens of congregations, chaplaincies, and other ministry settings, we have observed and learned from these fellow travelers, sisters and brothers who day in and day out serve faithfully among the people of God. As we have been privileged over the past two decades to teach, and serve in seminary administrative work, our faculty and staff colleagues have shared so many insights that are also woven into the fabric of this book. Above all, as many teachers will attest, one learns the most from the students who share classrooms, worship spaces, field study trips, and the breaking of bread accompanied by conversations both holy and hilarious!

Particular appreciation goes to colleagues who read all or parts of the manuscript and offered comments and suggestions that brought greater clarity and completeness: Rodney Hunter, Jean LeGros, Lauren Muratore, and Rodger Nishioka. We also express our thanks to David Schoenknecht, editor of the Fortress Foundations for Learning: Exploring Series, to production manager Marissa Wold, to all others at Fortress who had a hand in the project, and to colleagues writing other books in the series with whom we shared ideas along the way.

Pamela and Michael Cooper-White

# Introduction

> "Were not our hearts burning within us while he was talking to us on the road, while he was opening the Scriptures to us?"
>
> —Luke 24:32

Nearly thirty years ago, the story of Jesus and two fellow travelers on a path from Jerusalem to Emmaus (Luke 24:13-35) was the gospel reading we chose for our wedding. Having met and come to recognize each other deeply through the experience of accompanying pastors who had received death threats in El Salvador because of their advocacy for the poor, we identified with this story's themes. Rich in imagery, this passage from Luke is the story of a seven-mile journey that culminates in spiritual growth and recognition of God's presence in ordinary places among "regular people." As they move along on the journey, Jesus and his two companions share what has been happening in their lives, ponder the meaning of Holy Scripture, share their confusion and doubt, and move through the chaos to more clarity. As the journey concludes, the two who appear to reside in Emmaus extend hospitality to their fellow traveler; he accepts, and they break bread together in a holy meal. It is through these embodied practices—walking, hospitality, sharing a meal—that they recognize the Holy One in the midst of daily living and even in a time of suffering. Then when Jesus suddenly vanishes from their sight, they are empowered to go out and share with others what they have experienced.

Throughout the years, this short story of a brief journey has continued to captivate our attention. It encapsulates what we seek to share in the course of this volume in the Foundations for Learning series, *Exploring Practices of Ministry*. The very word *practice* is rich in meanings. Among other things, it implies that there is freedom to experiment, that we can continue to grow and expand both knowledge and abilities. That ministry is a practice means it is never perfected and never finished. As in a medical practice, we who engage in the art of ministry do so in community with others. All practices in this way are relational and contextual; they happen with and among other people and in a particular time, place, and culture. For this reason, practices are fluid and responsive to the social, political, and economic demands of the cultures and subcultures in which they are embedded. Practices of ministry, moreover, are not unaffected by dynamics of gender, race, sexual orientation, class, age, and physical ability, nor by the ways in which power and oppression have a disproportionate impact on persons, families, and communities. Practices of ministry, then, will always include aspects of advocacy for both mercy and justice.

Practices of ministry also do not occupy a separate sphere from theology per se. The core beliefs, doctrines, and play of ideas represented by the field of theology undergird and are continually refreshed and revised in the context of Christian practice. Theology without concern for life-giving practices and attention to the human condition (and indeed, all creation) is mostly an empty exercise of abstraction. Likewise, practices of ministry without reference to theological reflection may drift into secular professional models which, though by no means irrelevant, may not lift up the larger vocational purpose, or telos, of the Christian life: the equipping of all of God's people for their own ministries—their own unique callings from God.

As vocation, or calling, ministry is both different from and similar to other occupations. Among professions or occupations, it is unique in the broad array of forms through which "the ministry" is exercised—ordained pastors, priests, deacons, or bishops serving in congregations, synods, or dioceses, as well as those who serve under the title of "Reverend" as chaplains in hospitals, military services, or homes and facilities for the elderly or mentally and physically challenged individuals. Also serving in ministry are thousands of specially prepared individuals who remain among the laity (those not ordained) as they capably carry out many of the same tasks as do priests or pastors.

Given this breadth and diversity among those considering, preparing for, or already engaged in ministry, this short book cannot address every aspect of our callings. Rather, our aim is to offer readers a broad overview of the kinds of tasks many ministers fulfill and the ways they approach their vocations. We are also keenly aware of the wide range of theological and ecclesial traditions and denominational variations in perspective when it comes to how "the ministry" is understood. Our own social locations are within what are often described as "mainline churches"—Episcopal and Lutheran—and we are mindful that we see the world through the lenses of these traditions. As white professional-class North Americans, we also recognize the limitations of our perspectives in today's diverse pluralistic global family. Fortunately, however, both of us have had opportunities to work in a number of intercultural, ecumenical, and increasingly interfaith arenas, so our perspectives have been broadened and our own ministries greatly enriched by many fellow travelers from other traditions and backgrounds. Accordingly, we attempt to write for the widest possible readership, hoping that readers from all cultural contexts and in all traditions will find helpful guideposts along the journey through the chapters that follow.

Readers who seek herein a how-to manual or a kind of cookbook filled with recipes for successful ministries from proven practitioners will be disappointed! Think of it more as a tour guidebook pointing to significant ideas and places that you, the reader, must explore for yourself and integrate into your experiences. From our deep convictions that ministry is a journey with fellow travelers, and that each person's pathway is unique—with its own twists and turns, its special side roads and fascinating way stations—this book is intended as an opening to conversation and reflection, and includes something of our own experience. Between us, we have had the privilege of serving in a wide spectrum of calls throughout the years—as parish ministers, ecumenical church agency executives, and as seminary professors/administrators; Pamela has also served as a pastoral counselor/psychotherapist and minister of music, and Michael as denominational executive and volunteer chaplain in the U.S. Civil Air Patrol. While neither of us has spent extended periods as an overseas missionary, we have both been given wonderful opportunities to engage in international ministry contexts as consultants and visiting ministers/scholars in Latin America and Central and Eastern Europe. Gleanings from these personal experiences across our combined several decades of ministry are supplemented by our learnings from a vast array of colleagues and students who have shared their insights and wisdom.

## The Road Ahead: An Overview

In planning even a short road trip, we like to see the big picture on a map or engage the GPS function that provides an overview of the entire journey. This introduction, accordingly, will offer a brief synopsis of the six chapters that follow. Each chapter could be thought of as a logbook entry encapsulating one segment or dimension of the journey from Jerusalem to Emmaus.

In chapter 1, the journey begins with Jesus' question to his two fellow travelers: "What are you talking about anyway?" This introduction to the field of practical theology is authored primarily by Pamela, who teaches as a seminary professor of pastoral and practical theology. She builds upon Jesus' foundational question and goes on to explore theological method—how biblical, theological, and historical studies relate to ministerial practices like counseling, teaching, preaching, and engaging in social ministry and advocacy for justice. This chapter will help the reader grasp the critical importance of paying attention to the context in which a ministry is exercised, and to understand key theological terms and historical trends in practical theology.

The journey from big city to rural village was marked by a remarkable degree of honesty and truth telling. Jesus' companions did not shy away from a prophetic naming of the reality that the Messiah's crucifixion was at the hands of religious leaders and civic authorities. In their forthright prophetic confrontation, these travelers were "speaking truth to power." Chapter 2 of the book explores the challenging call to be proclaimers of the word, the truth that Jesus promised will set us free (John 8:32). We embrace the astounding claim that through our human words, the living Word of God—Jesus the Christ—comes alive in the church, which Martin Luther once called the "mouth house." Preaching, therefore, is serious business and demands careful preparation, including careful study of biblical texts, as well as the congregational and cultural contexts into which the word is delivered by our words. Some practical tips on sermon preparation, delivery, and gaining feedback and wisdom from one's listeners are also offered in the chapter.

Early in the trek from Jerusalem to Emmaus, Jesus prodded his companions to move beyond the disappointment and disillusionment that resulted from their limited perspectives. In admonishing them for their foolishness, he opened new horizons for their thought and action. Later, at table, he opened an entire new future as they recognized his identity—the dead one resurrected! In short, we see Jesus on the journey, at the table, and in his subsequent appearances as a steward of the mysteries in the gathered worshipping community, the topic of chapter 3. Whether ordained or lay, most who serve in a public ministerial vocation will have responsibilities that include "up front" dimensions. Ordained clergy will preside at worship, leading the faithful as they celebrate the sacraments and conduct other holy rites. Lay ministers of liturgy or music in a congregation, campus ministry, or other setting are agents of grace in a unique fashion. Both ordained and lay leaders will assist congregations and other groups through worship leadership and proclamation of God's realm of justice and peace with new insights through preaching and public speaking. Those who serve as chaplains or in administrative posts may have less visible roles, but they also are agents of grace in communities that may be short-lived but intense and fast-paced.

While on the journey homeward with the bewildered Emmaus citizens, Jesus may have appeared somewhat harsh in his confrontations. Reading a bit behind the text, however, we capture glimpses of his profound commitment and compassion for these dejected and disheartened travelers. In chapter 4, this central ministerial calling is explored from multiple perspectives, including individual, family, and wider contexts of care tied to public theology and social justice. A key for any who would provide support to and care for others is to cultivate the ability to use one's own reactions and responses care-fully, and to set one's own issues and agenda to one side at times, as we engage in a profound posture of active listening. Empathy and sensitivity, moreover, are not innate talents that we are either good at or not; they are intentional practices that can be learned and deepened. Pastoral-care providers must also recognize their own limitations and observe healthy boundaries. Part of this is to cultivate a network of other professionals in community to whom appropriate referrals can be made on a moment's notice.

In schools of education where various teaching methods are explored, a common assertion these days is that good pedagogy has shifted from the teacher being "sage on the stage" to her or his being a "guide on the side." This metaphor is obviously in sync with Jesus' modality in facilitating the continuing education of the two travelers on the road to Emmaus. Rather than lecturing them based on his authority as the resurrected Messiah, he prodded them by asking probing questions like this one: "Was it not necessary that the Messiah should suffer these things and then enter into his glory?" (Luke 24:26) Chapter 5 recognizes that a minister's teaching role is exercised in all kinds of venues. While ministers may indeed stand in a pulpit or at a lectern in a classroom on occasion, the majority of most ministers' teaching occurs in more informal settings—over lunch at a café, in parishioners' homes or hospital rooms, and on the streets for those who engage in ministries that are based in contexts involving community organizing or other social outreach. The chapter includes an overview of Christian educational philosophy, a summary of how persons progress developmentally through stages of faith, and innovative and liberating approaches to pedagogy and faith formation including children, youth, and adults of all ages.

At the conclusion of the journey story, after the two Emmaus dwellers recognized the identity of the fellow traveler who had set their hearts ablaze with fervor, they got it and recognized they could not just sit there basking in their reverie. They had to get on with the mission! So they scurried back to Jerusalem to share what they had experienced and to begin strategizing with the other disciples how their message might be spread far and wide. In any setting, regardless of one's exact title or job description, the practice of ministry involves organizational leadership and good administration. These topics form the core of the final chapter, which makes the case that administration is neither a necessary evil nor an afterthought, but rather part and parcel of incarnational ministry that occurs "in the flesh" (the real world that involves things like budgets, legal issues, strategic planning, personnel oversight, and the like). Beyond some practical suggestions, we seek to offer therein theological foundations that undergird a servant-leader lifestyle.

## Welcome to the Journey!

Regardless of where you may find yourself vis-à-vis the practice of ministry—from a prospective seminarian deciding whether or not to dip a toe in the waters of a theological education and formation process, to one well along the journey to ordained or public lay ministry, to a long-seasoned practitioner years or decades into the profession—we welcome you as a fellow traveler! Here in the early twenty-first century, there may be no more challenging and complex vocational calling than this one that we have accepted. Churches, religious institutions, ecclesial communities—by whatever name we choose to call the places where people come together out of faith perspectives—are under fire almost everywhere these days. Resources are limited and diminishing in many places. Even as religion is an intrinsic part of culture, the various "culture wars" and power differentials that exist in (our) North American society do not cease when people pass through the doors of a congregation or other gathering of people of faith. "Faith" itself means many different things to different people, and its varying expressions both overtly and covertly shape varying and at times conflicting practices of ministry. Some of the same polarizations that have fractured the public discourse are present in many faith communities. It is therefore often a crucial practice of ministry in a pluralistic society and world to stand in the breach as peacemakers, conflict mediators, and creators or even enforcers of bully-free climates of safety and hospitality for diversity.

While such an intense climate of change and challenge may deter some who in more tranquil times would embrace the practice of ministry, many (and we assume, from your taking this book in hand, that includes you!) are responding as did Isaiah, the prophet of old, "Here am I, Lord, send me!" (Isaiah 6:8) And in the final analysis, has there ever been a time of utter peace and tranquility in which people of faith have not been called to speak truth to some injustice and to bind up the wounds of the brokenhearted? So, replacing nostalgia with realism, we set off together on our own Emmaus road to discover Christ in the sometimes joyful, frequently challenging practices of talking and debating, extending hospitality to the disturbing stranger, and sharing generous fellowship at table. Let the journey begin!

# The Walk to Emmaus

## (Luke 24:13-35, NRSV)

[13] Now on that same day two of them were going to a village called Emmaus, about seven miles from Jerusalem, [14] and talking with each other about all these things that had happened. [15] While they were talking and discussing, Jesus himself came near and went with them, [16] but their eyes were kept from recognizing him. [17] And he said to them, "What are you discussing with each other while you walk along?" They stood still, looking sad. [18] Then, one of them, whose name was Cleopas, answered him, "Are you the only stranger in Jerusalem who does not know the things that have taken place there in these days?" [19] He asked them, "What things?" They replied, "The things about Jesus of Nazareth, who was a prophet mighty in deed and word before God and all the people, [20] and how our chief priests and leaders handed him over to be condemned to death and crucified him. [21] But we had hoped that he was the one to redeem Israel. Yes, and besides all this, it is now the third day since these things took place. [22] Moreover, some women of our group astounded us. They were at the tomb early this morning, [23] and when they did not find his body there, they came back and told us that they had indeed seen a vision of angels who said that he was alive. [24] Some of those who were with us went to the tomb and found it just as the women had said; but they did not see him." [25] Then he said to them, "Oh, how foolish you are, and how slow of heart to believe all that the prophets have declared! [26] Was it not necessary that the Messiah should suffer these things and then enter into his glory?" [27] Then beginning with Moses and all the prophets, he interpreted to them the things about himself in all the scriptures.

[28] As they came near the village to which they were going, he walked ahead as if he were going on. [29] But they urged him strongly, saying, "Stay with us, because it is almost evening and the day is now nearly over." So he went in to stay with them. [30] When he was at the table with them, he took bread, blessed and broke it, and gave it to them. [31] Then their eyes were opened, and they recognized him; and he vanished from their sight. [32] They said to each other, "Were not our hearts burning within us while he was talking to us on the road, while he was opening the scriptures to us?" [33] That same hour they got up and returned to Jerusalem; and they found the eleven and their companions gathered together. [34] They were saying, "The Lord has risen indeed, and he has appeared to Simon!" [35] Then they told what had happened on the road, and how he had been made known to them in the breaking of the bread.

## Chapter 1

# On the Road: Practices as Theology, and Theology as Practice

> Now on that same day two of them were going to a village called
> Emmaus, about seven miles from Jerusalem, and talking with
> each other about all these things that had happened.
>
> —Luke 24:13-14

At the outset of the Emmaus story (Luke 24:13-35), verbs describe the activity of Jesus' two fellow travelers: they were going, talking, and discussing. As Jesus entered the picture, his activities included accompanying (he came near and went with them" [v. 15]), asking questions, interpreting the Scriptures, and breaking bread at table. All these things might be conceived of as Jesus' and his companions' practices of ministry. They involved doing, but also thinking, talking, and reflecting in community.

---

**Practices of ministry** are more than a set of duties or skills! *Practices of ministry* are activities that intentionally bear the marks of Christian faith, are grounded in biblical and theological reflection, are relational, communal, and open to continual revision as the Spirit continues to prompt new responses to the needs of each new time and place.

---

Here at the beginning of our journey in this book, we pose the fundamental question: What are practices of ministry, and how do we understand them theologically? A basic definition would be simply that they are what ministers (both lay and ordained) actually do. We might expand the definition a bit further, however, and say practices of ministry are what ministers *do* and also what we *think* about how and why we do it. As Christian practitioners, we minister with practices that are grounded in Scripture and informed by the work of centuries of theologians who came before us. Practices of ministry are more than simply a set of skills, or even the application of the wisdom from theologians and practitioners from other disciplines (biblical studies, systematic theology, church history, psychology, sociology, educational theory, organizational theory, etc.) to our work in ministry. Practices of ministry, as noted in the introduction, do not exist apart from theology. Jesus himself was continually talking, teaching, and debating points of theology as he engaged in the practices of healing, feeding, and sitting at table with people from all walks of life. On the Emmaus road, as the disciples walked with the risen Christ, "beginning with Moses and all the prophets, he interpreted to them the things about himself in all the scriptures" (Luke 24:27).

Theology is a dry and dusty mental exercise indeed if it has no relevance for daily living! And ministers who get caught up in tasks without ongoing theological reflection can easily lose their spiritual and vocational moorings. We may think of theology exclusively as what we think and say—"words about God" is the literal meaning of theology, from *theos* + *logos* in the orig-

---

**All good theology is practical** in its import, and all Christian practices are theological. Our words about God imply a moral shaping of our actions, and our actions reflect (for good or for ill) our deepest beliefs. Because God is involved with us through both our practices and our believing, our intentional prayer and reflection on theology undergirds our practices of ministry, and our practices likewise inform and help to grow our faith and beliefs.

---

inal Greek—but theology is also something we enact. What we do is always undergirded by our own beliefs, whether these are made explicit or remain implicit even to ourselves. Whenever we act, we are communicating (even subliminally) what we believe God is like and how God is active among us. Perhaps some questions to ask, then, concerning all our practices as Christians would be: In what way is what I am doing helping to build up God's realm of love and justice (the "kingdom of God") here and now? Or is what I am doing a distraction from, even an obstacle to, what God desires for the world? (God's "desire" is another, perhaps more intimate and loving way of translating God's "will" from the original Greek *thélēma*.) How is what I am doing helping to equip others for their own ministries, helping to empower and facilitate their particular God-given gifts to serve God in this world?

In recent decades, there has been increasing attention to the whole concept of practices, both in theology and in other fields. The term *best practices* has become an important watchword for improving the quality of services in many professions. In academic scholarship in a range of fields, practices have been given new attention, as philosophers, political scientists, and others have begun to challenge the false dichotomy of theory and practice (as well as mind and body) inherited from the ancient Greeks.[1] Practices can be understood as more than mere activities or tasks. *Practices* as a technical term (from the Greek *praxis*) means constellations of activities that develop in communities as normative ways of behaving. Aristotle used the word *praxis* to mean not just action, but political activity, implying that it was an activity that shaped both individuals and society.[2] Practices both reflect and (re-)shape the values and aspirations of the surrounding culture. Practices imply standards of excellence, communally adopted to conform to ideals of what is good. More than mere procedures, practices are intended by communities to enhance life according to commonly shared values. As veteran educator and practical theologian Craig Dykstra has written, "Learning and carrying out some valuable practice provides, in itself, an important form of moral and spiritual education. Our powers are increased and our minds and spirits are enlarged. Not every activity is a practice in this sense. Painting is; shaving is not."[3] Dykstra refers to Christian practices as "habitations of the Spirit."[4]

In theology, an entire discipline called practical theology has seen a new surge of development, as teachers and scholars of the independent disciplines of pastoral care, preaching, worship, education, and leadership engage in the larger questions of how theology can inform and be informed by what Christians encounter in everyday life and how we respond to human situations of pain and brokenness. This growing interest in practical theology was spurred in part by a growing interest in the late twentieth century among so-called systematic or constructive theologians in considering what wisdom might be gleaned from non-theological sources such as science, psychology, and philosophy. This issue of which sources carry sufficient authority for discerning what is "right," "true," or "salvific" has been a central concern of theologians, especially since the Protestant Reformation.

> **Practical theology** is the discipline in which systematic, constructive theology and our practices as baptized persons meet. Practical theologians do constructive theological thinking that relates directly to the practices of care and counseling, worship and preaching, education and formation, leadership and evangelism, and all forms of daily practice as Christians in response to the needs of the world.

Theologians from different branches of the Christian family have emphasized different sources, including Scripture, tradition, reason, and experience. Those in the Protestant tradition, beginning in the sixteenth century, emphasized Scripture alone (*sola scriptura*), while those in the Catholic tradition maintained the importance also of tradition—the accumulated deposit of theological knowledge and wisdom from the earliest church onward. Anglicans and Methodists explicitly adhered to the conviction that our sources of wisdom also include God-given reason and experience. Around the globe today, many Protestants also stress the centrality of experience in their personal relationship with Jesus Christ and acceptance of the Bible as a direct guide for living. The distinctions among various traditions' use of sources, however, are seldom absolute, as most Christians utilize both their own and others' reflections to help interpret what they read in Scripture. Jesus' own discussion with the disciples on the road to Emmaus incorporated all of these: he drew on their shared scripture and inherited theological traditions ("Moses and the prophets"), and he engaged in the reasoned interpretive practices he had learned from the time he was a child seeking out the rabbis in the synagogue (Luke 2:46-51), until experientially their "hearts were burning within them." (Luke 24:32)

Interest among theologians in beefing up the dialogue between the wisdom of the church and the wisdom of the world became a significant subject of debate and elaboration in the twentieth century. The famous theologian Paul Tillich nearly scandalized some of the more traditional theologians with his notion of "correlational theology"—that the immediate concerns of the world (the literal meaning of the word *secular*) should be "correlated" with theology. For Tillich, this was still mostly a one-way street: the world posed questions, especially existential or ultimate questions about the meaning and purpose of life and the problem of suffering, and theologians were tasked with providing answers that were both appropriate within the established boundaries of Christian thought, which Tillich called the "Christian message"), but also adequate to addressing the human situation.[5] This claim was further elaborated by theologian David Tracy, who asserted that this correlation needed to be a *two*-way street, in which both the theological traditions of the church and the secular disciplines such as philosophy and the social sciences could raise questions—including mutual critique—and both could offer answers.[6] This correlation entailed two criteria (or norms) for determining what was good theology: adequacy for and appropriateness to both the Christian tradition and the human situation. Tracy called this approach to theology "mutual critical correlation." More recent theologians have pressed this idea further, even questioning the division between theology and the world as a false dichotomy, and demanding critical self-reflection on the part of the theologian.[7]

## Where We Start Shapes the Journey

One important distinction can be made between practical theology (and other theologies that emphasize Christian life and practice) and the long European tradition of "systematic" theology. This has to do with the disputed arena of theological methodology—simply stated, the starting points (sources), criteria (norms), and accepted ways of going about doing theological thinking (methodology). The main distinction might be understood as a difference in methodology between *deductive* and *inductive* ways of formulating theological concepts. Deductive thinking works from a prior theory or proposition and employs some forms of testing and analysis to arrive at a conclusion that (one hopes) corresponds to some dimension of reality. Inductive thinking, in contrast, begins with an aspect of lived reality or experience and works its way up through some forms of testing and analysis to a more generalized description or theory. Deductive thinking tends to conform more to the scientific method (beginning in the eighteenth century with the Enlightenment), even in nonscientific fields of study, and looks for measurable evidence in empirical data or other sources to support a hypothesis. Inductive thinking tends to conform more to humanistic approaches to understanding the meaning people make of their experience, and often rejects scientific "neutrality" in favor of ethical, social, and even political inquiry into lived phenomena.

> **Practical theology begins from the ground up.** That is, it takes as its starting point the human condition, and the current situation being addressed (including individuals, families, communities, societies, nations, and the whole creation), and puts those in dialogue with scripture and the historical theological tradition. It does not begin, as some theological reflection does, with an abstract idea or proposition about the nature of God apart from the living creation now. It frequently engages issues of justice and healing as related theological themes for action.

While the following is a pretty large generalization, the European theological tradition, which from the nineteenth century was influential in the United States, can generally be thought of as a deductive approach. Its sources were first the Bible and then the theological teachings of the early church fathers (sometimes called the study of patristics, mostly without reference to the church mothers of the time!), through prominent saints and "doctors of the church" such as Augustine of Hippo (354–430 CE[8]), and Thomas Aquinas (1225–1274). Continuing on through leading luminaries of subsequent centuries in the West—especially, for Protestant theologians, the great Reformers of the sixteenth century Martin Luther (1483–1546) and John Calvin (1509–1564)—this culminated in an effort in the nineteenth and twentieth centuries to produce very large "systematic" theologies intended to address every possible question about God, Christ, creation, humanity, the church, sin, and redemption.

Well into the last century, brilliant theologians labored to produce multivolume systematic theologies, many of which continue as foundations of modern theological work today—for example, Paul Tillich's *Systematic Theology* (three volumes),[9] Karl Barth's *Church Dogmatics* (fourteen volumes!),[10] and Karl Rahner's one-volume *Foundations of Christian Faith*.[11]

These authors worked within many traditional categories of thought from early Christianity, with a focus on inherited doctrines, in an effort to offer new and timely interpretations. Following the tradition of Aquinas and other great medieval summae (summations) of doctrine, their aim was to create a logically coherent and comprehensive statement of doctrine within their own theological tradition (e.g., Lutheran, Reformed, Roman Catholic). The medieval European style of disputation and academic critique was carried on into the twentieth century, as theologians debated competing formulations. While the ultimate goal of such work was to help guide both Christian belief and faithful living, the accent was on the propositional level of belief.[12]

In the twentieth century, both practical theologians and theologians who operated within the discipline of systematics began to question the primacy of working at this propositional level. From a number of different directions, theology began to change from a deductive to a more inductive approach. In the aftermath of the catastrophic violence of the Holocaust and the unleashing of the atom bomb, people in both the academic world and the public square began to question authority (including both institutions and beliefs) in unprecedented numbers. In Europe, particularly in Germany, a massive postwar disruption and collective guilt became the soil out of which grew a movement called "political theology," in which themes of suffering, justice, and hope became central.[13]

In the United States, the unsettling of prewar societal assumptions gave rise to the empowerment of formerly disenfranchised groups and individuals to speak up and raise questions. The civil rights movement, the movement for women's liberation, and the protests against the Vietnam War generated new critiques of both church and society. Theology as a discipline underwent a radical shift as women and scholars of color entered the field in growing numbers and began to question both its contents and methodologies.[14] No longer content to believe what was handed down "from on high," these new scholars began to claim the inductive authority of their own experiences of oppression. They mined ancient biblical and theological texts for evidence against sexism and racism, and created new theological approaches in which issues of power and domination were lifted up as central concerns. In recent times, liberative theological methods have been further extended to address the inequities perpetrated against sexual minorities, children, aging adults, and the disabled.[15]

## Voices from the Margins Expand the Conversation

Globally, important critiques were also being raised up from the margins of power. In Latin America, in response to the church's complacency and collusion with oppressive regimes, a powerful movement called liberation theology developed in which theology was no longer the province of ordained priests and trained theologians, but open to everyone. Latin American priests and theologians in the 1960s created "base communities" in urban barrios and rural villages, in which people read and interpreted the Bible for the first time from the lens of their own (often marginalized) experience. These theologians found in the life and teachings of Jesus a strong warrant for the assertion that God stands in solidarity with the disempowered and shows a "preferential option for the poor."[16] *Mujerista* (Latina feminist) theologian Ada María Isasi-Díaz further articulated the importance of daily life (*lo cotidiano*), drawing on women's experiences of care and justice, as the ethical foundation for not just right belief (orthodoxy) but right practice (orthopraxis).[17] Asian theologians have interrogated culturally conditioned shame (in Korean, *han*) and cultivated new theologies from the underside of Confucian-influenced social and ecclesial hierarchies.[18]

While highly controversial among some more traditional theologians, this theological pronouncement further inspired Black, Asian, and African theologians to claim their own theological voices and to develop theologies that would speak meaningfully to their own social and political situations. Womanist (Black feminist) theologians draw on the power of survival and resistance against multilayered oppressions to inform theology and practices of ministry.[19] Today, theologians increasingly represent racial, ethnic, and gender diversity across the globe. Many write from a "postcolonial" perspective—that is, a perspective that recognizes the historical reality of colonization (which often went hand in hand with Christian missionary evangelization) but at the same time claims the authority of precolonial indigenous beliefs and practices, and the power to create a new and emancipatory version of Christianity that emerges uniquely from their distinctive contexts.[20]

This may seem like a long side trip from practices of ministry, but it is actually highly relevant, because as theology shifted in large part from deductive to inductive methods—to valuing human experience as a source of authority for truth alongside or even radically equal to the Bible and the inherited traditions of theological thought, as in the work of Black theologian James Cone[21]—the importance of what Christians actually do in the world became far more central to the theological project overall. Practical theologians have embraced these changes and made them central to their work. We spend a good deal of time in our writing and conferences discussing theological methodology, precisely because we stand in a new relationship to the old propositional style of doing theology. Perhaps the best way forward, as so-called systematicians and practical theologians meet at the crossroads of scholarship and everyday life as Christians and citizens, is to recognize that both deductive and inductive methods have a place in theological reflection. However, the fundamental starting point for practical theology will always be the reality of human experience, with a particular accent on human suffering (and by extension, the brokenness and suffering of all creation). And practical theology is always driven by a goal of transformation of unjust systems, the flourishing of creation, and living in eschatological[22] hope toward the coming of God's reign of peace and justice in this embodied, earthly life.

Practical theologians, then—coming from specific fields of study including homiletics (preaching), pastoral care, Christian education, and a variety of ecclesial (churchly) disciplines exploring leadership, evangelism, and mission—are generally no longer content merely to apply received dogma, but as of the later twentieth century claimed the authority of practices themselves to instruct and inform theological reflection. And from the other side of the aisle, many systematic theologians are likewise deconstructing the abstract nature of traditional theology, arguing that to be meaningful, theology must have relevance for Christian life and practice.[23] The ancient Greek philosopher Aristotle distinguished among different kinds of knowledge, including *technē* (technical how-to knowledge or craft), *epistēmē* (scientific knowledge or knowledge of facts), and *phronesis* (usually translated as practical wisdom).[24] For Aristotle, *phronesis* involved character and values, and an ability to understand how to act ethically in society. *Phronesis* goes beyond the mechanics of *technē* (although it's certainly still important to have a set of skills that allow us to perform tasks with care and excellence) and is also more than mastery of information. In the same way, practical theology defines the various fields of ministry practices as more than either technical ability or book learning, as crucial as both of those are to understanding how to minister faithfully and well.

There are many **types of knowledge**: technique, the grasp of facts, and wisdom. Practical theology engages all three, but emphasizes **wisdom**, which integrates all of these, and carries with it the comprehension of ethical values and practices.

Practical theologians claim the authority of our experience as ministry practitioners to build theology from the ground up and to engage in theological imagination that remains close to what human beings actually need in a variety of contexts and settings.

## Being a Theologian-Practitioner: A Circular Dance of Wisdom

Practical theologians are almost always theologian-practitioners, equally steeped in both theology and the closely related secular field(s) to which their practices refer for both theory and technical skills. For example, pastoral caregivers are thoroughly trained in clinical psychology; professors of church and society are grounded in the study of ethics and sociology; homileticians are trained in writing, rhetoric, and oratory; ministers of music are highly trained in music theory and performance; professors of leadership and evangelism are well studied in the arts of organizational development, finance, and even marketing! It is perhaps a natural move, then, for theologian-practitioners to demand that theology and practice be in continual mutual dialogue.

One of the leading practical theologians of the twentieth century, Don Browning, articulated a method that has guided the field in recent decades.[25] Just as the grassroots theologians in the Latin American base communities wove together personal experience with scriptural interpretation, Browning advocated for a "practice-theory-practice" model, in which theological thinking begins first with the immediate pastoral situation, using sound social scientific principles to understand as deeply as possible what is happening, bringing this together with moral and theological reflection (for example, on what God might be doing in the situation and how we might be called to act), and then choosing an appropriate pastoral response guided by this thinking process. Each action, each new immersion in the human situation calls for further reflection, and each moment of reflection informs further practice.

Practical theologian and educator Richard Osmer characterizes this not just as a linear triangle, but an ongoing spiral,[26] involving four interlinked tasks of practical theological interpretation: the descriptive or empirical ("gathering information that helps us discern patterns and dynamics in particular episodes, situations, or contexts"), the interpretive ("drawing on theories of the arts and sciences to better understand and explain why these patterns and dynamics are occurring"), the normative ("using theological concepts to interpret particular episodes, situations, or contexts, constructing ethical norms to guide our responses, and learning from 'good practice'"), and the pragmatic ("determining strategies of action that will influence situations in ways that are desirable and entering into a reflective conversation with the 'talk back' emerging when they are enacted").[27] Educator Thomas Groome developed a similar pattern of action and reflection in his Shared Christian Praxis model.[28]

Working from a postcolonial perspective, Emmanuel Lartey has raised cogent critiques of earlier approaches.[29] To the extent that traditional West-

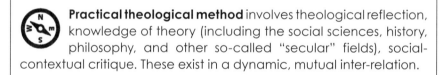

**Practical theological method** involves theological reflection, knowledge of theory (including the social sciences, history, philosophy, and other so-called "secular" fields), social-contextual critique. These exist in a dynamic, mutual inter-relation.

ern theology viewed practices as derivative applications of systematic theology, it perpetuated a "second-class citizenship" for the practical disciplines. More process-oriented (or clinical) approaches ran the risk of devolving into anti-intellectualism. Lartey has proposed a "learning cycle for liberative pastoral praxis" that incorporates the practice-theory-practice model but adds the necessary further step of applying a more robust situational or contextual analysis and critique to the theological reflection itself (see figure 1.1).[30]

Lartey's work, deriving from his experiences in his native Ghana, Africa, as well as Europe and the United States, highlights another crucial dimension of practical theology: that of community as the primary location for practical theology. Inasmuch as practical theologians begin with the human situation as the starting point for theology, with a particular emphasis on the alleviation of human suffering, this very emphasis has

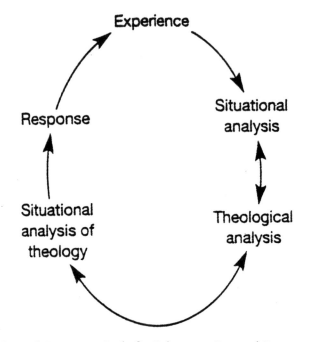

**Figure 1.1** Lartey's Learning Cycle for Liberative Pastoral Praxis

Source: Emmanuel Lartey, *In Living Color: An Intercultural Approach to Pastoral Care and Counseling,* 2nd ed. (London: Jessica Kingsley, 2003), 132.

helped to shift practical theology from an individual(istic) endeavor to one that is increasingly communally based. African theologian Mercy Oduyoye works exclusively within the context of a circle of women theologians, who view collaboration and mutual critique as essential for authentic theological work.[31]

While those of us who teach and learn in seminaries are obviously still committed to the idea of formal theological education, it should also be noted that the wisdom of practical theology is never a purely academic project. Nor does all good theology—practical or otherwise—come only from those with multiple diplomas and degrees on their walls. If we are to take seriously the premise that practical theology begins with the depths of human experience, then it is the experience of being human that finally grounds all our practical theologizing. Dorothy C. Bass, who has done much to articulate what practical theology does as a field, offers these reflections on the wisdom she has observed over many years among the laity:

Countless deliberations that reflect the kind of knowing pursued by practical theology have taken place, simply because those who found themselves set free to walk in newness of life have had to figure out how to move their feet along an unfamiliar path they could see only by the light of Christ and could navigate only with the help of the Holy Spirit. Disciples in [my] congregations have considered how to be generous with their money, how trusting to be of new acquaintances, and how to worship God in spirit and in truth. They have preached and listened and prayed and studied, often when facing challenges that were urgent and perhaps even life-threatening. They have learned to pray with, live with, care for, and mourn the death of a Christian brother or sister from a different cultural background. Not all, not even most, of their thinking has been cognitive; some seem to know what to do almost spontaneously, others seem to lurch along by trial and error, and still others engage in long, earnest conversations. But their thinking has been theological, nourished by Scripture and made possible by a lively, daring confidence in the grace of God. And it has been practical, improvising faith's music within a unique, terrible, and beautiful corner of this world so loved by God.[32]

Finally, we can return to the opening premise of this chapter—that practical theology is concerned with what Christians actually do. It is immersed in the immediate concerns of both church and world, and does not see those as separate realms. Practical theologians probe the depths of the biblical witness, the writings of theologians throughout the ages, and the expertise of secular research, theory, and professional competencies in order to meet the pastoral needs of people and congregations where they are. In following Jesus' mandate to feed the hungry, give drink to the thirsty, welcome the stranger, clothe the naked, care for the sick, and visit those in prison (Matt. 25:35-36), we are living into the practices to which our baptisms as Christians have called us. As we have stated in the introduction to this book, all Christians are called to ministry, not just the ordained. And as practitioners of ministry, we are also all theologians. Practical theology gets down and dirty with some of the toughest problems in this beautiful but broken world. We are not called as Christians to lives of careless comfort, but lives of care-full attention as God's hands and feet in the world. To recall an oft-quoted line from the writer Frederick Buechner, "Neither the hair shirt nor the soft berth will do. The place God calls you to is the place where your deep gladness and the world's deep hunger meet."[33]

Practical theology can therefore be quite a messy business—and probably that's when it's at its best! To turn to another story of Jesus' appearance to the disciples after his death and resurrection, in John's Gospel (20:24-29), the disciple Thomas is often portrayed by preachers as a wimpy, wavering doubter. But we prefer to view him as perhaps the most courageous and bold among the disciples. Only Thomas ventured out when others remained huddling in fear behind closed doors. And only Thomas was encouraged by the Resurrected Crucified One to plunge his hand deep inside his still-unhealed wounds. Thomas was one who was willing to roll up his sleeves and got his hands dirty.

Thomas was a practical theologian who recognized that the practice of ministry involves both joy and sorrow, high moments of fellowship with Jesus and one another followed by painful engagement with the world's suffering. Thomas was unafraid to live into profound theological questions like "Who is God, and how can a loving God allow such dreadful things to happen?" At the same time, Thomas was willing to act before all questions were answered to his satisfaction. Thomas's story invites us to go deeper in our own explorations of what it means to be engaged in the messy, sacred practices of ministry.

##  Questions for Personal Exploration

1. As you ponder the "voices from the margins" in our world today, who comes to mind? Are there ways in which you see churches engaging respectfully with those who live at the margins of society?

2. Many persons and groups claim to have *the* truth regarding complex social and political issues. As a practical theologian, how will you distinguish between multiple truths claimed by Christians (and others)? What are some of the guiding principles by which you might analyze situations and seek to act in accord with God's compassion and love?

3. Craig Dykstra says that not every activity is a "practice" in the sense of a "habitation of the spirit." ("Painting is; shaving is not.") What would you identify as some of your deep practices?

4. In this chapter, we have described both deductive (from doctrines) and inductive (from experience) methods of doing theology. Which method resonates best for you and why?

5. Where in your current life situation can you imagine Lartey's cycle of practice and contextual analysis (see Fig. 1.1) might be useful to you right now?

 ## Resources for Deeper Exploration

Bass, Dorothy C., and Craig Dykstra, eds. *For Life Abundant: Practical Theology, Theological Education and Christian Ministry.* Grand Rapids: Eerdmans, 2008.

Cahalan, Kathleen A., and Gordon S. Mikoski, eds. *Opening the Field of Practical Theology.* Lanham, MD: Rowman and Littlefield, 2014.

Lartey, Emmanuel. *Postcolonializing God: New Perspectives in Pastoral and Practical Theology.* London: SCM, 2012.

Miller-McLemore, Bonnie, ed. *The Wiley-Blackwell Companion to Practical Theology.* Malden, MA: Wiley, 2014.

Woodward, James, and Stephen Pattison, eds. *The Blackwell Reader in Pastoral and Practical Theology.* Oxford: Blackwell, 2000.

 ## Notes

1. For a more detailed discussion of this, see Bonnie Miller-McLemore, "Introduction: The Contributions of Practical Theology," in *The Wiley Blackwell Companion to Practical Theology*, ed. Bonnie Miller-McLemore (Malden, MA: Wiley, 2014), 1–4.

2. For more on the meaning of *praxis*, see Thomas H. Groome, *Sharing Faith: A Comprehensive Approach to Religious Education and Pastoral Ministry: The Way of Shared Praxis* (San Francisco: HarperSanFrancisco, 1991), 133–38. Groome also cites Aristotle's *Ethics.*

3. Craig Dykstra, foreword to Maria Harris, *Fashion Me a People: Curriculum in the Church* (Louisville: Westminster John Knox, 1989), 9–10, drawing on Alasdair MacIntyre, *After Virtue* (Notre Dame, IN: University of Notre Dame Press, 1981), 175.

4. Craig Dykstra, *Growing in the Life of Faith: Education and Christian Practices*, 2nd ed. (Louisville: Westminster John Knox, 2005), 63–64.

5. Paul Tillich, *Systematic Theology*, vol. 1 (Chicago: University of Chicago Press, 1951), 3–68.

6. David Tracy, *Blessed Rage for Order: The New Pluralism in Theology* (New York: Seabury, 1975).

7. Notably, Mark L. Taylor, *Remembering Esperanza: A Cultural-Political Theology for North American Praxis* (Maryknoll, NY: Orbis, 1990).

8. You are probably familiar with the common abbreviations BC for "before Christ" and AD for "*anno Domini*," meaning "the year of our Lord." You will encounter an alternative way of designating these eras of history in biblical and religious studies, which avoid Christian exclusivism: BCE for "before the common era" and CE for the "common era" (in which we now live).

9. Paul Tillich, *Systematic Theology*, 3 vols. (Chicago: University of Chicago Press, 1951–57).

10. Karl Barth, *Church Dogmatics*, 14 vols., ed. Geoffrey W. Bromiley and Thomas F. Torrance (London: T. & T. Clark, 2004; orig. pub. 1961).

11. Karl Rahner, *Foundations of Christian Faith: An Introduction to the Idea of Christianity* (New York: Seabury, 1978).

12. For a nuanced discussion of the differences and similarities between practical and systematic theology today, see Serene Jones, "Practical Theology in Two Modes," in Dorothy C. Bass and Craig Dykstra, eds., *For Life Abundant: Practical Theology, Education, and Christian Ministry* (Grand Rapids: Eerdmans, 2008), 195–212.

13. For a good overview, see Peter Scott and William T. Cavanaugh, *The Blackwell Companion to Political Theology* (Malden, MA: Blackwell, 2006); Rebecca Chopp, *The Praxis of Suffering: An Interpretation of Liberation and Political Theologies* (Maryknoll, NY: Orbis, 1986).

14. For example, James Cone, *A Black Theology of Liberation*, 2nd ed. (Maryknoll, NY: Orbis, 1997); Rosemary Radford Ruether, *New Woman, New Earth: Sexist Ideologies and Human Liberation*, 20th anniversary ed. (Boston: Beacon, 1995).

15. For example, Richard Cleaver, *Know My Name: A Gay Liberation Theology* (Louisville: Westminster John Knox, 1995); Joyce Ann Mercer, *Welcoming Children: A Practical Theology of Childhood* (St. Louis: Chalice, 2005); Fredrica Harris Thompsett, *Courageous Incarnation: In Intimacy, Work, Childhood, and Aging* (Cambridge, MA: Cowley, 1993); Nancy Eiesland, *The Disabled God: Toward a Liberatory Theology of Disability* (Nashville: Abingdon, 1994).

16. A term coined by Gustavo Gutierrez and adopted at the widely influential Latin American Bishops' Conference at Medellín, Colombia, in 1968.

17. Ada María Isasi-Díaz, *En la Lucha/In the Struggle: Elaborating a Mujerista Theology*, 2nd ed. (Minneapolis: Fortress Press, 2003).

18. For example, Kwok Pui Lan, *Introducing Asian Feminist Theology* (Maryknoll, NY: Orbis, 2000); Andrew S. Park, *The Wounded Heart of God: The Asian Concept of Han and the Christian Doctrine of Sin* (Nashville: Abingdon, 1993).

19. E.g., Delores Williams, *Sisters in the Wilderness: The Challenge of Womanist God-Talk* (Maryknoll, NY: Orbis, 1993); Emilie Townes, ed., *Embracing the Spirit: Womanist Perspectives on Hope, Salvation, and Transformation* (Maryknoll, NY: Orbis, 1997); Katie G. Cannon, *Katie's Canon: Womanism and the Soul of the Black Community* (New York: Continuum, 1995).

20. For example, Emmanuel Lartey, *Postcolonializing God: An African Practical Theology* (London: SCM, 2013); Catherine Keller, Michael Nausner, and Mayra Rivera, eds.,

*Postcolonial Theologies: Divinity and Empire* (St. Louis: Chalice, 2004); Lamin Sanneh, *Disciples of All Nations: Pillars of World Christianity* (Oxford: Oxford University Press, 2007).

21. Cone, *A Black Theology of Liberation*.

22. Another fifty-cent theological word, referring to the hope for the fulfillment and perfection of creation by God at the promised end-time (in Greek, *eschaton*). For a concise and compelling discussion of eschatology in relation to pastoral theology, see Jürgen Moltmann, "Eschatology and Pastoral Care," in *Dictionary of Pastoral Care and Counseling*, ed. Rodney Hunter and Nancy Ramsay, 2nd ed. (Nashville: Abingdon, 2005), 360–62.

23. For example, Edward Farley, *Theologia: The Fragmentation and Unity of Theological Education* (Minneapolis: Fortress Press, 1983); see also Farley, *Practicing Gospel: Unconventional Thoughts on the Church's Ministry* (Louisville: Westminster John Knox, 2003).

24. Aristotle, *Nichomachean Ethics*, 2nd ed., ed. Lesley Brown, trans. David Ross (Oxford: Oxford University Press, 2009).

25. Don Browning, *A Fundamental Practical Theology: Descriptive and Strategic Proposals* (Minneapolis: Fortress Press, 1991). See esp. pp. 1–9.

26. Richard Osmer, *Practical Theology: An Introduction* (Grand Rapids: Eerdmans, 2008), 11.

27. Ibid., 4.

28. Thomas H. Groome, *Sharing Faith: A Comprehensive Approach to Religious Education and Pastoral Ministry* (San Francisco: HarperSanFrancisco, 1990), 135–427; Groome, *Christian Religious Education: Sharing Our Story and Vision* (San Francisco: Harper & Row, 1980).

29. Emmanuel Lartey, *In Living Color: An Intercultural Approach to Pastoral Care and Counseling*, 2nd ed. (London: Jessica Kingsley, 2003); Lartey, "Practical Theology as a Theological Form," in *The Blackwell Reader in Pastoral and Practical Theology*, ed. James Woodward and Stephen Pattison (Oxford: Blackwell, 2000), 131–32.

30. Lartey, *In Living Color*, 132.

31. Mercy Amba Oduyoye, *Introducing African Women's Theology* (Sheffield, UK: Sheffield Academic, 2001).

32. Dorothy C. Bass, "Ways of Life Abundant," in Bass and Dykstra, *For Life Abundant*, 40.

33. Frederick Buechner, "The Place God Calls You To," Frederick Buechner Center blog, January 11, 2013, http://frederickbuechner.com/content/place-god-calls-you (quoting from Buechner, *Wishful Thinking*).

## Chapter 2

# Setting Hearts on Fire: Practices of Proclamation

> "Were not our hearts burning within us while he was talking to us on the road, while he was opening the scriptures to us?"
>
> — LUKE 24:32

The Emmaus travelers' astonished recognition of what had occurred in Jesus' presence with them on the road and at table point to the heart and soul of our calling as public ministers: prophetic proclamation of the word of God, and gracious hosting of a community when it gathers for worship. In this chapter, we will explore a number of themes related to preaching, including not only how it brings to bear the word of God for members of a congregation or individuals who receive pastoral care but also how prophetic preaching can have a powerful impact in broader public circles. Chapter 3 will focus more on the practice of ministry within the gathered church community, wherein ministers serve as "stewards of the mysteries," leading worship, conducting rites and ceremonies, and presiding at the sacraments.

Among all the tasks involved in being a public minister, perhaps none causes as much anxiety for most contemplating or preparing for this calling as preaching. Seminarians may sweat over parsing Greek verbs or dread an upcoming exam in systematic theology, but preaching that first sermon before a professor and peers in a preaching class may cause palpitations of the heart and a week of sleepless nights! In general, many if not most would-be ministers may be reticent at public speaking. But even experienced professionals who may have been teachers, regular public speakers, or even orators in prior careers (for example, lawyers, business executives, politicians, or military officers) may tremble at the prospect of crafting and delivering the unique address that is the sermon or homily.

One of the daunting aspects of preaching is that the task is never done. At sunset on Sunday, after a long day of leading worship, conducting classes, tagging along with a youth group, or making emergency hospital visits, a preacher may reflect back on the morning's sermon and conclude, "I hit it out of the park today!" And then, for the preacher as for the ballplayer, the stark reality sets in: "And I have to start tomorrow morning getting ready for next week's game." Beyond the unrelenting rhythm wherein Sundays come around much faster for preachers than other people is the reality that the impact, the effectiveness of one's preaching is so difficult to measure. At the door after the service, a limp handshake and the comment "Nice sermon" don't convey much. In contrast, a parishioner who comments on a particular point that was made—even if he or she disagrees or has questions—helps us to know we connected. And both of us have had the experience of not feeling a sermon was very inspired or inspiring until members of the congregation made such specific comments of appreciation that we realize the Holy Spirit really does get involved in this mysterious process!

While most clergy tend to rate themselves as strong if not superb preachers on their professional profiles that are made available to parish call or search committees, we probably all have our moments of self-doubt when we question, "Am I really adequate to this awesome task?" Entering the pulpit to guest-preach one Sunday, Pamela was a bit daunted to see a sign prominently taped to the lectern: "We would see Jesus." Try living up to that! The very popularity and growing pool of resources on preaching—the steady stream of published "preaching helps" books and journals, along with the plethora of websites, workshops, and conferences on preaching—attest to preachers' felt need to get better at this most challenging dimension of our calling.

## Church as Community of word and Word

Martin Luther once referred to the church as a "mouth house," in recognition that the spoken human word is a primary means by which the divine word of God becomes known. To be sure, a phrase attributed to Saint Francis, "Preach the gospel; if necessary use words," likewise holds true in that God's will and ways are often best reflected in actions rather than words. Nevertheless, sooner or later, words must be used to interpret God's and faithful people's actions. Human speech itself constitutes an action, as when a judge or jury utter one word, "guilty" or "innocent," as when the umpire declares "ball" or "strike," or as when one authorized declares, "I pronounce you husband and wife," or "I declare your sins are forgiven."

The apostle Paul recognized the constitutive nature of Christian proclamation and the unique role of those who proclaim the word when he asked in Rom. 10:14, "And how are they to hear without a preacher?" By the time Paul wrote this most comprehensive epistle to the Romans, preaching to both believers and the general public had a history. Christian preaching stands in continuity with the prophetic tradition of the Jewish and other peoples, wherein prophets like Isaiah arose within the community to declare, "Thus saith the Lord." Jesus' ministry was characterized by its continuity with the rabbinical tradition of teaching in intimate settings with his disciples, but increasingly he also addressed large crowds (the "multitudes") in extended declarations that can be regarded as sermons. In the immediate aftermath of the crucifixion and resurrection, those who came to be known as the apostles rose to their feet and began declaring the gospel and how it must henceforth shape the lives of those who believed. Upon their return to Jerusalem from Emmaus, the two who had journeyed and dined with the risen Christ "told what had happened on the road" (Luke 24:35)—that is, they gave their testimonies in a public declaration. Luke, who alone among the gospel writers records the Emmaus story, goes on in the book of Acts to note that immediately following Jesus' ascension, "Peter stood up among the believers" (Acts 1:15) and began to preach. In his various lists of gifts provided by the Spirit to the people of God, Paul cites "prophecy and exhortation" (Rom. 12:6-8), "the utterance of wisdom and knowledge" (1 Cor. 12:8), and the gift of being "prophets, evangelists, pastors and teachers" (Eph. 4:11).

From the outset, accordingly, the church has always been a wordy community dedicated to passing along from one generation to the next the word of God, and to expanding the circle of those given opportunity to consider the claim that "Christ is risen!" Among the many forms in which the divine word is communicated by human words, preaching is unique and remains viable, even essential today amidst a context revolutionized by twenty-first-century technology. Reading collections of sermons from different historical periods reveals that, as with most things, this dimension of ministry practice is marked by both continuity and change. In some regards, the basic structure of a sermon—which includes an introduction, conclusion, and typically one or more themes or key points in between—remains the same as when the first Christian preachers delivered their messages two thousand years ago. But in other ways—the illustrations and examples used to convey meanings, the rhetorical forms employed, and increasingly the use of contemporary technological and multimedia devices projected onto a big screen before the congregation—twenty-first-century preaching would be unrecognizable to those who first heard the gospel by means of a first-century sermon.

Learning to preach and growing more effective as the years go by, therefore, involves finding the proper balance between continuity and innovation. Seasoned teachers of preaching will attest that they go about their task differently than a decade or two ago. They must help students understand how those who attend church and listen to sermons have changed: many are now much less familiar with the Bible and "churchy" language than previous generations were. At the same time, the ultimate aim of preaching today remains the same as when the first apostles invented the "job description" for a gospel communicator—as Luke put it at the outset of his Gospel proclamation, "So that you may know the truth concerning the things about which you have been instructed" (Luke 1:4).

## Preaching: Art or Craft? Both and More

Can a preacher be considered a craftsman or craftswoman? Is learning to preach like acquiring the skills to build a house from the ground up or perform a complicated surgery—where textbook learning and observation of proficient masters at work lead to gradually assuming more and more of the responsibility, first under close supervision and then practicing independently as a fully credentialed expert? Many have suggested that "the art of preaching" is a more apt descriptor of the nature of proclamation than viewing preaching as craft (or *technē*; see chapter 1). In our opinion, dimensions of both art and craft are involved in preparing and delivering sermons. A good preacher must find ways to let creative juices flow, see the world in ways most people do not, get the right angle or aspect as does a photographer or painter, select the right motif as does the writer, determine the best medium as does the sculptor, and hear the music in one's head as does a composer. Developing one's artistic abilities as proclaimer is as difficult and elusive for would-be preachers as honing creative edges is for artists in other arenas. As a musician must practice, practice, practice and a painter must keep applying brush to canvas, so too the gospel proclaimer must simply keep preaching, preaching, preaching!

A key to cultivating artistic proclamation is giving careful attention to the use of language. In her short book *Creative Preaching: Finding the Words*, the late Elizabeth Achtemeier spoke of the importance of seeking to become a master of words:

> A preacher's tools are words, shaped into the rhythms and cadences, the fortissimos and whispers, the conversation and confrontation of oral speech. To neglect the mastery of words is to be like a carpenter who throws away his saw and sets out to fashion a piece of fine furniture, using nothing but an ax. We may hack away at a congregation with tools totally inappropriate to their purpose—dull words, misleading sentences, repetitious paragraphs, ineffective illustrations. Or we may take up the fine tool of language, honed and polished to a cutting edge, and then trust that God will use to fashion his people. . . . The committed preachers—the faithful servants of God—do not neglect their tools![1]

While recognizing the artistic elements required, most professors of preaching (also called "homiletics") will assert that any homily or sermon includes certain structural elements, just as a building project follows a pattern of laying a foundation, erecting the superstructure, roofing, placing conduits and lines for utilities, completing interior construction, and completing the job with painting, flooring, and other finishing touches. At bare minimum, a sermon includes an introduction, conclusion, and assertions (some would say even "arguments") in between. It is typically a blend of illustrative scriptural quotes and references; stories, vignettes, or accounts of personal experience; and theological statements about the nature of God and how God's word may be speaking to our contemporary situation and demanding some response from the hearers.

In some traditions, the theology or piety surrounding preaching may regard the preacher as a directly inspired mouthpiece for the Holy Spirit.

**Homiletics** is derived from a Greek word meaning "to assemble and be in conversation," thereby pointing to the importance of a preacher's striving to help listeners engage in making meaning together. While "homily" often connotes a brief message, any sermon can rightfully be called by that name. Academic study of homiletics in a seminary involves students not only in actual sermon preparation and delivery, but in thinking critically about the nature of the preaching task, pondering matters of rhetoric as well as biblical interpretation, and thereby developing a solid foundation for a lifetime of faithful proclamation.

While neither of us has experienced in any profound way a sense of being "taken over" by the Spirit in the pulpit, we do not discount colleague preachers who describe such occurrences. But even those who subscribe to a more charismatic (Spirit-inspired) understanding of the preaching task also pay attention to key elements of the preaching craft like good enunciation and voice projection, avoidance of offensive words and images that distract listeners, and the use of summations that lodge key points in the sermon listeners' hearts and minds.

## The Sermon as Crossroad Conversation

"Stop preaching at me!" "Now you're preaching!" Retorts like these emanate from children to parents, from students to teachers, and often, perhaps good-naturedly, among friends. But even when uttered lightheartedly and half-jokingly, they reveal the typical person's resistance to being preached *to* or *at*. To avoid such a reaction and acknowledge that, as Luther said on his deathbed, "We are all beggars" (including those who stand in the pulpit), we preachers do well to conceive of the homily or sermon as conversation rather than orally delivered dissertation. Conversation involves mutual exchange of perspectives and careful listening to one another. In the charismatic tradition, it is not unheard of for a parishioner to jump up midsermon and proclaim an opposing point of view, saying, "The Lord has laid it on *my* heart to say. . . ." Both the preacher's voice and the parishioner's are taken seriously. Even in traditions where less spontaneity is the norm, a sermon can take on a participatory nature by inviting parishioners to study the biblical texts together with the preacher. Occasionally, two or more preachers can engage in a "dialogue sermon" or an interpretive reenactment of a biblical text from the pulpit.

As a theological conversation, a sermon or homily includes not only a preacher and her or his listeners; we believe and claim that God's voice joins the dialogue as well! Since a central objective of any Christian sermon is to re-present the One who was crucified in order to launch the reign of love and justice in the entire cosmos, this particular discourse can be described as a cross-road conversation. Its ultimate purpose is to point both preacher and listeners along the cross-bound road to Calvary. The sermon is also a crossroads conversation in that it occurs at the intersection of sacred text (Scripture), a particular context (place and time), a given community (congregation), and the preacher's personhood, meaning the sum total of who one is as a gifted but flawed, divinely beloved yet still imperfect human being.[2]

Coming to grips with one or more biblical texts stands at the heart of preparing to preach. If a sermon gives voice only to personal opinions of the preacher or merely offers commentary on some contemporary issue or another, it may well impart wisdom, offer counsel and encouragement, and even inspire, as does any good speech or public address. But it will not reliably proclaim the word of God. Regardless of how one's particular Christian tradition describes and places the Bible's authority alongside reason, tradition, scientific exploration, etc. (see chapter 1), all churches regard Holy Scripture to a high degree as the "authoritative source and norm of proclamation, faith and life."[3] Studying a text of Scripture is often referred to by the Greek word *exegesis*, which means simply "to draw out." As a preacher begins to engage with the text, this drawing out ideally involves studying in the original language of Greek or Hebrew, or at least seeking out the nuances that may occur in the original text through use of biblical commentaries that set forth various alternative meanings of a word or phrase. Courses in Bible and hermeneutics help prepare seminarians or divinity school students for this all-important work of grappling with a text. For texts that appear in multiple variations in the Bible (for example, many of the parables and sayings of Jesus included in two or more of the four gospels), a comparison of similarities and differences in the various versions will reveal additional insights regarding a particular biblical author's perspective and intent. (And no, the Bible does not have a single author! A quick survey of the entire table of contents of the Christian Bible shows that it was written across many centuries in varying locales, using different genres—story, history, song and poetry, proverbs, letters, and prophetic visions. It is best thought of as a library rather than a book.) Broadening the study to understand where a particular text sits in its larger context is part and parcel of what is commonly referred to as the historical-critical method of biblical interpretation. And as one begins to imagine how a text might speak to one's particular community in this moment of the long sweep of history, reading recent sermons by one's contemporaries on a text may be an additional helpful measure of preparation.

***Hermeneutics*** comes from a Greek word meaning "to interpret." Theologians refer to a "hermeneutical gap" that exists between ancient worldviews reflected in biblical texts and our contemporary perspectives. Hermeneutics, therefore, involves the multi-layered work of asking, "What did these words or phrases mean back then? How have they been understood during various historical eras, and what do they mean for us in our time and place?"

Another critical instrument that we have come to understand as essential in any exegete's toolbox is described by feminist and liberationist biblical scholars and theologians as the hermeneutics of suspicion. Among other things, this phrase points to the reality that the bulk of Christian history writing, preaching, and authoring the great tomes of theology whereby the faith has been transmitted through twenty centuries comes from men, and European white males in particular. A new wave of scholars who have broadened hermeneutical perspectives immeasurably over the past half century have argued convincingly that because so many texts have been interpreted through these men's limited spiritual lenses, traditional interpretations must be approached with a measure of wary suspicion. Many unchallenged and long-cherished understandings based upon Scripture must be deconstructed; great theological edifices constructed over centuries, like some of the magnificent European cathedrals, sometimes must be torn down in order to find a lowly cow stall where the true Savior was born! All interpreter-preachers must recognize that we see the world (including Scripture) from the vantage point of our particular social location, which is inevitably limited. Accordingly, a thorough and "thick"[4] or multilayered involvement with a portion of Scripture should involve attempts to see it through the eyes of those who are very different from ourselves. For those of us in North America and much of Europe, it is important to read the commentaries and sermons of African, Asian, and Latin American theologians. Even better for a preacher in search of holistic interpretation is to engage in conversation with persons from diverse backgrounds to gain their understandings and learn how a text speaks to their experience.

> **Exegesis** comes from Greek words that mean "to guide, lead or draw out." The person who engages in the work of drawing out meanings from a text can be called an *exegete*. By means of careful study and analysis a text is viewed through multiple lenses that consider its grammar and structure in the original language, usage in various historical periods, comparison with similar texts, and placement within broader portions of Scripture. Exegesis is sometimes contrasted with *eisegesis,* which means "to read into" a text one's own predisposed interpretations and conclusions.

No less critical a skill than reading and exegeting a biblical text well is the ability to "read the context" and exegete the culture of the congregation or community in which one is called to serve. While some who minister will be lifted up as leaders within congregations where they have been members for many years, most of us begin a new ministry as relative strangers or outsiders. While it can be a challenge at first to serve a congregation that feels a bit strange or alien, there is an advantage as well in approaching a community with fresh eyes that can see some things longtime residents take for granted or overlook.

In recent years, a growing area in seminary curricula is often described in academic catalogs and course listings under the heading of "congregational studies." Those who teach and write in this field of study recognize that, no matter its size or location, any congregation's culture is complex and multivalent. Congregational culture is profoundly shaped by the place in which a given people of God gather. By this we do not mean exclusively or even primarily the building or worship space, though that too will have a significant impact on a congregation's ethos and liturgical life. The larger societal context deeply affects a faith community's lifestyle and shapes its mission. Getting to know a church's context and understanding its culture—both internal and external (the dominant culture of the surrounding social context)—are, therefore, important priorities both at the outset of a new ministry and on an ongoing basis as the congregation and its larger community keep changing over time.

To become an effective "gospeler" for a particular gathered community, a minister might think of her- or himself as an anthropologist who as a "participant-observer" asks a series of fundamental questions: Who are these people? What are they like? What language do they speak? (Even within an apparently monolingual grouping, there are ranges of accents, local catch-phrases, and idioms.) How do they think of themselves and of those they regard as "others"? What are their communication patterns and the most effective media and messaging by which to reach them? For them as a community, what key moments along the way have shaped their history? What are their taboos, and what practices are held sacred and inviolable, at least by some groups within the congregation (as in "We've always done it that way!")? Where are neuralgic points, sensitive nerves, and forbidden zones? What touches their hearts and brings them their greatest joy?

In classes at our respective seminaries, we encourage students to explore the nature of relationships between individuals and groups in a congregation. This approach sometimes is described as viewing a family, congregation, or other organization through the lens of a "systems" perspective (see chapter 4). Observing who relates to whom, how groups interact with one another, and how power and authority are conferred begins to reveal a congregation's culture or way of being. How are differences of gender and sexuality negotiated (overtly or covertly)? What is the place of children? And how are "outsiders"—particularly those of different race, ethnicity, or economic status from the majority group(s) in a congregation—welcomed, held at bay, or even feared and rejected? Who are viewed as leaders, and how are their roles understood? Does one have to be a longtime member to be elected to the governing body, or are relative newcomers also embraced in selecting leaders?

By now, the reader may be wearying of all these questions, protesting, "Do I really have to act like a private detective before I can preach and lead worship?" On the Emmaus road journey, before Jesus began to teach (and as Luke portrays it, probably preach!), his primary way of interacting with his two fellow travelers was to ask simple, basic questions: What are you discussing? (Tell me about your recent history and the ways in which it affected you so deeply. How exactly did you experience those horrific moments in Jerusalem when your beloved friend was executed? What meaning are you making of all that has occurred?) In short, Jesus was reading the context and seeking to discern what German biblical scholars first described as the *Sitz im Leben* (life circumstances) of his hearers. As disciples of Jesus in our time, an important dimension of our vocation is to be students of the communities and contexts in which we are called to serve.

In some contexts marked by rapid turnover in the population of those served, "preaching to a parade" may be an apt metaphor. This is particularly true in communities with a high percentage of students, military personnel, or immigrants en route to more permanent locations. It is obviously also the case for ministers who serve as hospital, jail, or nursing home chaplains. Under such circumstances, a key ability required for effective proclamation is that of establishing rapport and a pastoral relationship within a brief period of time. Unlike those who serve in communities of greater stability, those who minister in these contexts seldom see the long-term impact of their ministries. Similarly, those of us (like seminary professors and administrators, denominational executives, and bishops or supervising ministers) who are regularly invited as guest preachers must endeavor to read a context from a distance and with limited information. When so invited, the authors seek to gain understandings of a congregation or other community through studying its website, asking questions of colleagues who may know the context, and inquiring of its current leaders what concerns and issues might be paramount in people's lives.

A final comment regarding attention to context in preaching involves the reminder to see and address the big picture. While one always preaches in the midst of a particular community, with its unique constellation of persons, issues, and culture, that local community exists within the larger world. While all may be tranquil at home in Yourtown, all hell is breaking loose somewhere else in the world, causing great suffering and death to sisters and brothers in the human family. In their pathbreaking book, *Liberation Preaching: The Pulpit and the Oppressed*, Justo and Catherine González remind us of the necessity of paying attention to the big-picture context, especially those they describe as "the powerless who are absent" in most middle-class congregations:

> This means that part of the task of preaching, as well as part of the preparation for it, is to ask the question, how would this biblical text be heard and applied authentically by someone in a radically different political and social setting? It is not only the preacher who needs to be aware of such interpretations in order to develop a more adequate theology; the congregation needs to develop the same skill in order to discover more adequately its mission in the world and how that mission can be carried out.[5]

As we prepare for the preaching moment, having grappled with the appointed or chosen text(s), following the sociological and anthropological efforts to more fully exegete the context and grasp the culture of a congregation or other community of the faithful, the remaining partner at the crossroads is ourselves. "And how are they to hear without someone to proclaim him [Christ]?" asked Paul in Romans 10:14. The late Herman G. Stuempfle, who taught generations of Lutheran preachers at Michael's alma mater, Gettysburg Seminary, wrote of the preacher's being the "living reality—the host of the dynamic interchange between text and context, pericope[6] and people."[7] Unless one simply reads or presents the sermon of another (which in our opinion should be rarely if ever done—and not without attribution), Stuempfle names the reality that "It is from within our consciousness as preachers that the sermon is generated. In our own being we provide the womb for the birth of a new form of the Word of God."[8]

While, as we stressed at the outset of this chapter, a sermon that can rightfully claim to be the word of God can never be simply a string of the preacher's personal opinions, those who come to hear us do seek assurances that we really believe what we are saying. Our listeners will deem us authentic proclaimers of good news only if they sense that it brings joy and inspiration to us personally and impels us to outreach and service. Does this mean that every sermon includes some dimension of what is often called personal testimony? By no means do the authors believe that the words *I* or *my* should be sprinkled generously throughout every sermon! To the contrary, our own sermons and those of many we regard as outstanding preachers tend to be somewhat sparing in this regard. If a personal story or insight is relevant, feel free to share it (being careful, however, if the story involves others—including family members—to seek their permission). But as Pamela's preaching mentor Krister Stendahl warned his students at Harvard Divinity School, somewhat tongue-in-cheek, "If you have a genuine religious experience, do not share it more than five times total in your preaching career."[9]

The point was, of course, that old stories about ourselves may become set pieces that do not encourage us to grow beyond them—and they also may become self-aggrandizing. The more important dimension here, however, is to seek in every way to be fully present as a member of the community gathered at the crossroads to hear the word of God. This involves such skills as knowing your material well enough to look at people (either individuals or sections of the congregation at a time) and using appropriate language and images that communicate, "I really care about you and want you to understand." The preacher's personal authenticity can also be enhanced by seeking feedback, asking in essence, "Am I getting across? Are my sermons helpful? How might I better address your concerns and sufferings, and celebrate your joys with you?"

Another dimension of the preacher's personhood, which is readily discerned by listeners, is her or his courage to "speak truth to power."[10] As preaching may take on a more prophetic dimension, those who hear will grasp whether the preacher is timid or bold—one who is willing to stand up and take the heat from those who may disagree or one who quickly retreats in the face of conflict and criticism. We were blessed to become acquainted with Lutheran pastor Robert Koons prior to his death at an advanced age. We soon learned a story that circulated about his prophetic preaching during the civil rights struggles of the 1960s. Koons had recently accepted a call to a prominent pulpit in a southern city when the tragedy of Martin Luther King's assassination occurred. He quickly called together a small group of the parish lay leaders and posed the question, "How might your new pastor address this tragic event in this week's sermon?" The parish leaders immediately blurted out, "Don't say anything at all, Pastor, it will just cause conflict if you raise this hot-button issue in church." No doubt in his warm, gentlemanly way, Koons just responded firmly, "Well, I can see you did not understand my question. It's not an option to say nothing. I asked you *what* I might say and how I might speak at this crisis moment in our nation's history."

Another among our many mentors in the practice of boldly proclaiming the word, including its prophetic calling to justice and peacemaking, was Bishop Stanley Olson, Michael's bishop and boss while serving on a synod staff in California. At every minister's service of installation where he was invited to preach, the bishop would say to the congregation, "On this day as your new pastor begins her or his ministry, I want you to think about the day you should ask her or him to leave you and go elsewhere. That day will come when you find yourself going home from church each Sunday and always agreeing with what the pastor said in the sermon!"

One rarely makes a weekly or yearly plan that includes, "Be a prophetic preacher on Wednesday," or "Set the nation back on its heels to reexamine its prejudices and oppressive ways during the month of May." (In fact, preaching only about certain issues—for example, about domestic violence during October as Domestic Violence Awareness Month or about racial justice during February as Black History Month—tends to marginalize such issues and fence them off from "regular" sermons.) The opportunities and privileges of being prophetic proclaimers tend to surprise us, and often we resist mightily this dimension of our callings. At such times, we need to be reminded that the road we traverse is a cross-road, that the One we proclaim is the Crucified God,[11] and that the very integrity of our personhood and ministerial authenticity hinges on our willingness to preach the whole word of God, including its prophetic and unsettling aspects.[12]

## Preparing, Practicing, and Preaching a Sermon

One of the questions that seminarians most frequently ask their professors and practicing parish clergy is, "How do you go about preparing a sermon?" To that age-old question there are probably as many answers as there are preachers. Even though we may have studied with the same homiletics professor and read the same books on preaching, we all go about it in our own unique ways. When it comes to sermon preparation, therefore, we cannot offer readers a surefire, tried-and-true how-to instruction. We are reluctant to propose the kind of formulaic approach to sermon preparation offered by some homileticians.[13] What we can do is offer a few "vectors" that might point in the directions one could go, based upon our own experiences and those of colleagues, including authors whose works on the art and craft of preaching require considerable shelf space in any seminary's library and occupy rapidly expanding bandwidth for delivery on the Internet as well.

Among decisions to be made at the outset is the type of sermon to be delivered on a given occasion. Will this week's sermon be primarily a teaching or pedagogical lesson on a biblical text that without interpretation is obscure, confusing, and even troubling? Is my primary objective in the upcoming Sunday's homily to inspire, or to bring focus on a vexing contemporary issue in the congregation or the local or global community? Has destructive behavior on the part of congregants risen to the level it simply cannot be avoided in preaching? Under such circumstances, an exhortatory sermon may need to offer a measure of reproof, even a call to repentance followed by the assurance of God's forgiveness. (We urge caution here based upon experience that highly critical sermons are often experienced as the preacher's launching a grenade, and the preferred approach to dealing with conflict under most circumstances is a more dialogical and conversational setting in which all parties immediately may share their feelings and opposing perspectives.) Also falling under the banner of sermon type is whether the message will be delivered in "ordinary time" (a regular Sunday that does not mark a major festival) or on one of the high feast days, as they are often called, like Christmas, Easter, Pentecost, or the days in commemoration of a saint of the church (ranging from the ancient church fathers and mothers to Martin Luther King Jr. and Oscar Romero).

Beyond the regular Sundays and other liturgical holy days, a typical working parish preacher will be called upon for untold numbers of special homilies that are included in weddings, *quinceañera* celebrations, home blessings, and other happy occasions, as well as the sad moments that mark funerals and memorials. In the case of the latter, in particular, there may be limited time as one squeezes in sermon preparation alongside caring for a grieving family and conducting all the regular work of a typical week in the parish. Some helpful brief texts published in recent years can assist beginners as well as experienced preachers in pondering the dynamics of what are often referred to as "special-occasion sermons."[14]

In preaching, as in other practices of ministry, preparation for and later evaluation of a task or encounter may be aided by developing a brief written or mental "impact profile." This discipline involves asking oneself this simple question: What is the intended (or at least hoped for) impact or outcome of my work in this instance? In the case of sermon preparation, completing the sentence "By means of this sermon, I intend to . . ." can focus the preacher's mind, help shape an outline, and determine a sermon's type, length, format, and even delivery style. As many listeners have attested, a preacher who never varies the style—means of communicating, way of making points, and even posture or gestures—can quickly become boring and be tuned out. While there is something artificial about standing in a pulpit or walking about the chancel in an empty sanctuary with no one present, practicing one's delivery can be helpful in two ways. First, repeated rendition of the sermon lodges it in memory and helps the preacher avoid reading or being tied to a manuscript. In addition, such oral rehearsal may also reveal (since the ear can at times hear what the eye cannot discern) content inconsistencies, awkward or confusing phrases, and repetition that a congregation is best spared. Besides, since the preacher on Sunday morning tends to be preoccupied with what's coming next in the service, a distracting child, or an unexpected development, the time of sermon rehearsal alone in the sanctuary may be the best opportunity for the preacher to personally hear the good news being delivered!

Among the aspects of delivery style are such considerations as whether one stands in a pulpit or wanders about in a chancel or even among the people. In recent decades, the trend in this regard seems to be the latter, with more preachers abandoning the pulpit for a "up close and personal" preaching position. As we have previously counseled, each preacher has to discover her or his own comfort level with various communication methods and styles. A counterpoint to the noticeable trend toward informality and interactive delivery is sounded by Lucy Lind Hogan in her book *Graceful Speech*. Not downplaying at all the importance of body language and paying close attention to "how one moves, stands and gestures" in front of a congregation. Hogan nevertheless raises a caution about how congregations receive those who "wander as they preach." In many cases, she reports, parishioners don't like such an informal delivery style: "They want them to stand in the pulpit . . . so that they can see them and hear them."[15]

Out of curiosity, in a congregation where the norm at the most family-oriented service was to deliver the sermon down on the floor at the head of the center aisle, Pamela sat in the back pew one Sunday as her colleague preached. What she immediately realized was that the preacher *feels* more connected—but only to those in the first few pews! Those farther back could not even see him. But sometimes parishioners also want their preachers in the pulpit because "that is where the preacher stands to deliver the Word of God. In this moment the preacher's concept of who a preacher is, the fellow traveler, conflicts with the congregation's conception of a preacher as the leader."[16] Hogan's book contains a wealth of wisdom about the use of one's voice, choice of language, utilization of the arts and technologically generated images to accompany preaching, and decisions regarding use of manuscript versus notes or a bare mental outline, as well as both traditional and creative contemporary "homiletical habits."

## Seven Parting "Commandments" for the Practice of Preaching

As with each practice addressed in this brief book, so much more could be said about the all-important calling of those who, when asked to stand and deliver the word, respond with Isaiah, "Here am I; send me!" (Isa. 6:8). We will conclude the chapter with seven brief words of encouragement to cheer on those already preaching as well as readers who still await their first appearance in a pulpit.

1. Thou shalt be diligent, steadfast, and faithful. Amidst all the busyness of every minister's life, plan adequate preparation time. At the same time, avoid being overprepared to the extent that the sermon seems old hat to you and will be received as the same by your hearers.

2. Thou shalt not be boring. The secret to avoiding staleness and remaining an ever-green preacher will differ for each secret seeker. Our experience suggests that one key is a belief in and commitment to the fundamental value of lifelong learning. Continuing to read, see movies, and explore interesting tributaries on the wide river of the Internet will help a preacher and her or his sermons remain interesting over the long haul.

3. Thou shalt not steal (and this means others' materials). Whereas in prior generations, one seldom if ever even considered the possibility of pla-giarism in preaching, the omnipresence of homiletical material a few keystrokes away on the Internet has led to multiple scandals in recent years. It can also lead to such gaffes as beginning a sermon with "When I was the archbishop of Canterbury" (unless, of course, thou *art* the arch-bishop of Canterbury!). If a congregation cannot trust their preacher not to "kidnap" (the literal meaning of the root word for *plagiarize* in Latin) another's material in preparing to teach and preach, they will not trust the minister in any other dimensions of her or his calling.[17]

4. Thou shalt not be overly repetitive (in one sermon and in the longer sweep of proclamation). We all have our pet themes, biases, and strongly held convictions. Repeating them week after week, regardless of whether or not these opinions bear any relation to the appointed or chosen scriptures, can result in a congregation's feeling harangued and questioning whether they are hearing God's life-redeeming and world-changing word or only the same old words of their pulpit tenant.

5. Thou shalt not presume that PhDs are legion in the pews, nor that "the masses" merit only pabulum. In even the smallest gathering of folk, there will be a range of ages, educational backgrounds, and familiarity with the Bible and Christian nomenclature and symbols. And even when one is preaching in a highly academic context like a seminary chapel, among learned professors, the sermon is a time for sharing faith together as children of God, not a time to impress with theological jargon or to give a scholarly lecture! Seeking to appear erudite by means of choosing archaic or obscure vocabulary, stringing together long, unpunctuated dependent clauses, and other complexities likely will impress only a few, if that, and will leave most listeners scratching their heads and looking forward to their Sunday dinner. At the same time, dumbing down a sermon shows disrespect to faithful people who have come to be fed, who may be more willing to be stretched than you give them credit for. The constant striving to find the proper balance in terms of tone, content, style, and delivery is the preacher-craftsperson's and preacher-artist's career-long challenge.

6. Thou shalt strive to be poetic. Not every preacher is or ought to be a published poet. But the artistic, metaphorical, and imagistic dimension of effective preaching requires an unremitting desire to be stretched, to cast one's glances farther and wider, to repeatedly be willing to be led by others, especially those very different from oneself, outside the comfort zone.

7. Thou shalt know when it's time to quit. We have all probably witnessed the restlessness that ripples through an entire congregation when a preacher goes on and on and seems incapable of concluding a sermon that began with some promise. While timing varies according to tradition, culture, and local custom, no one will be sad if you are so concise that your sermon runs a little short. Trimming redundancies is always a good practice.

A key to remaining vibrant in preaching and the entire practice of ministry is remaining healthily engaged in the entire practice of ministry. This involves a disciplined life of prayer, seeking (even demanding, since it can be so hard to receive sometimes) collegial support, engaging in dialogue with congregation members beyond the sermon moment, and in all regards keeping one's heart open so that the One who travels at our side can set it ablaze over and over again!

 Questions for Personal Exploration

1. As you contemplate preaching and other ways of proclaiming the gospel, what most excites you? What causes you the most anxiety or concern?
2. Is has been said that most preachers proclaim the same three sermons over and over. How would you avoid this trap of focusing overly much on your favorite themes and agendas?
3. Think of a congregation with which you are familiar. What have you learned about its ethos and "social location," and to what extent does the preaching address the people in that place?
4. To which passages of Scripture might you wish to apply a "hermeneutics of suspicion," and from whose perspective(s)?

 Resources for Deeper Exploration

Craddock, Fred. *Preaching.* 25th anniversary ed. Nashville: Abingdon, 2010.
Hogan, Lucy Lind. *Graceful Speech: An Invitation to Preaching.* Louisville: Westminster John Knox, 2006.
Lose, David J. *Preaching at the Crossroads: How the World—and Our Preaching—Is Changing.* Minneapolis: Fortress Press, 2013.
Taylor, Barbara Brown. *The Preaching Life.* Lanham, MD: Rowman & Littlefield/Cowley, 1993.
Tisdale, Nora Tubbs. *Prophetic Preaching: A Pastoral Approach.* Louisville: Westminster John Knox, 2011.

## Notes

1. Elizabeth Achtemeier, *Creative Preaching: Finding the Words* (Nashville: Abingdon, 1980), 22.
2. The "intersection" or similar imagery for a sermon occurs in multiple publications. Among them is Herman G. Stuempfle, *Preaching Law and Gospel* (Minneapolis: Fortress

Press, multiple editions), in which he points to "three living realities in sermon preparation": the word of scripture, the congregation, and the preacher (see chapter 6).

3. This description of the authority of the canonical Scriptures appears in the Confession of Faith of the *Constitution, Bylaws, and Continuing Resolutions* of the Evangelical Lutheran Church in America (available at www.elca.org and from Minneapolis: Augsburg Fortress).

4. Lucy Lind Hogan, *Graceful Speech: An Invitation to Preaching* (Louisville: Westminster John Knox, 2006), 81, drawing on the cultural anthropologist Clifford Geertz's term "thick description."

5. Justo L. González and Catherine G. González, *Liberation Preaching: The Pulpit and the Oppressed* (Nashville: Abingdon, 1980), 100.

6. This word is from the Greek, meaning a section or "cutting," and refers to a portion of Scripture that typically contains a complete story or key concept.

7. Herman G. Stuempfle, *Preaching Law and Gospel* (Minneapolis: Fortress Press, 1978), 81.

8. Ibid.

9. Krister Stendahl, "Ten Commandments for Preaching," class handout, Harvard Divinity School, spring 1982.

10. The origin of this widely-used phrase is unclear, but it has appeared frequently among Quakers, most prominently in a pamphlet issued in the 1950s: "Speak Truth to Power: A Quaker Search for an Alternative to Violence."

11. German theologian Jürgen Moltmann wrote a book of systematic theology by this title (Harper & Row, 1974), and the book remains worthy of careful study by preachers four decades after its publication.

12. For an excellent collection of essays on prophetic preaching, including serious engagement with various ethnic and cultural perspectives, see Christine Marie Smith, ed., *Preaching Justice* (Cleveland: United Church Press, 1998). An additional resource that explores proclaiming good news to those she describes as "encountering handicappism, ageism, heterosexism, sexism, white racism and classism" is Christine M. Smith's *Preaching as Weeping, Confession, and Resistance: Radical Responses to Radical Evil* (Louisville: Westminster John Knox, 1992).

13. For those who may want such a step-by-step—or in this case, day-by-day leading up to Sunday—approach to sermon preparation, see Paul Scott Wilson, *The Practice of Preaching*, 2nd ed. (Nashville: Abingdon, 2007).

14. See, for example, Susan K. Hedahl, *Preaching the Wedding Sermon* (St. Louis: Chalice, 1999); Charles Hoffacker, *A Matter of Life and Death: Preaching at Funerals* (Cambridge, MA: Cowley, 2002); Robert G. Hughes, *A Trumpet in Darkness: Preaching to Mourners* (Minneapolis: Fortress Press, 1985); Thomas Long, *Accompany Them with Singing: The Christian Funeral* (Louisville: Westminster John Knox, 2013), 183–97.

15. Hogan, *Graceful Speech*, 187.

16. Ibid., 40.

17. We are indebted to Hogan (ibid., 56–58) for the etymological insight and also commend her additional insights in the chapter on "The Virtuous Preacher."

# Chapter 3

# Stewards of the Mysteries: Practices of Worship

> While they were talking and discussing, Jesus himself came near
> and went with them.
>
> —LUKE 24:15

The road from Jerusalem to Emmaus was a public thoroughfare. While we might imagine that Jesus and his two companions chatted in hushed tones to keep their conversations private, nothing in Luke's account of the journey suggests that this is so. In fact, as their discussions became more animated, was it not likely that others on the road with them overheard bits and pieces when within earshot? We do not know how the details of their conversations were transmitted to the gospel writer, but it is clear that their exchanges on the Emmaus road were preserved and passed along, and ended up a central story near the conclusion of Luke's account.

The public nature of the Emmaus road story is consistent with the whole of Jesus' ministry. While the gospels recount times when he huddled with the disciples or was at table chatting quietly with friends in a private home, the bulk of his ministry was carried out in the presence of crowds made up of strangers. The better known he became, the more those in power—both civil authorities and religious leaders—were threatened. Seeing ominous signs on the horizon, his disciples tried to get him to back off and adopt a lower profile. "Don't go there," was Peter's response when Jesus foretold that his destiny was to be tried, convicted, and executed at Jerusalem (Matthew 23). But Jesus was not to be deterred; his life ended in a horrific execution in a high-profile place where the dying Savior became a public spectacle. In short, Jesus' ministry was a thoroughly public ministry.

Another marker of Jesus' lifestyle was its communal nature. To be sure, there were brief and extended periods when he went off on his own for prayer and contemplation. Frequently, the gospels tell us, Jesus escaped from the crowds and his disciples for a few hours, heading off to a place of retreat for communion with God and to recharge and refocus. His longest solo sojourn occurred just before he launched his public ministry, when he was alone in the wilderness for forty days, sorely, fiercely "tempted by the devil." (Luke 4:2) But following Jesus' victory over all the external arrows and internal doubts that the tempter threw his way while he was on his own in a desert place, the remainder of Jesus' ministry was in the company of a growing cadre of friends and fellow travelers. While on the road, he was constantly teaching, healing, counseling, and cajoling them to embrace a lifestyle marked by freedom, service to others, joyful camaraderie, and high-level fellowship.

In every way possible and under all circumstances, including amidst high tensions and gut-wrenching conflicts, Jesus' communal public ministry was marked as well by his profound and unshakable self-identity as life-giving servant. "I came that they may have life, and have it abundantly" (John 10:10) was his personal mission statement! He recognized that an abundant life is centered in God and regular conversation with the Divine through both personal and communal prayer. So he taught his disciples and the general public how to pray and how to worship rightly, "in spirit and truth" (John 4:24). He understood that holy living involves being engaged with holy things and spending time in sacred places. As an adolescent, he startled his parents and others by staying on in the Jerusalem temple among the priestly elders after his family and friends had departed on their homeward journey. It seems as if, at a young and tender age, he recognized the value of being in a place of worship where God was adored by the faithful. Later, when he launched his ministry as a roving rabbi, Jesus was constantly about opening the Scriptures to his disciples and the broader general public. So, too, his public ministry was marked by careful listening, offering forgiveness and absolution when he heard another's burden of guilt, and extending a healing touch when he discerned that so doing would make a difference in a person's life.

At first glance, it might appear that those we describe as being "public ministers" are primarily or even exclusively individuals typically referred to as priests, pastors, or ordained ministers. Certainly, such individuals (and we two are among them) play a central role in leading faith communities, particularly as congregations gather for worship, rites and sacraments. But in addition to those who typically bear the title Reverend, many others also serve as leaders in gathered communities. No lesser ministries are exercised by assisting ministers, lay Eucharistic hosts who extend the community's table to homebound or shut-in persons, ministers of music, and laity who may from time to time offer homilies and lead Bible studies. It is vital that those preparing for a variety of ministries be firmly grounded in these dimensions of the practice of ministry. Above all, we who bear responsibilities and exercise privileges of leading God's people at prayer and worship should be ever mindful of our calling to serve, in Paul's words, as "servants of Christ and stewards of God's mysteries" (1 Cor. 4:1).

## Exegeting a Community's Context and Culture

Among the multitude of tasks that a worship leader fulfills, reading and interpreting texts from Scripture and other sources on occasion is an obvious one. Since that which is read constitutes the word of God, developing the ability to read with clarity and accuracy is essential. Beyond the basic task of reading a text (where the reader in some congregations is listed in the bulletin as "lector"), offering interpretation by means of a homily or sermon is called for as well. Prior to such public proclamation of the word, the preacher, teacher, or rabbi needs to engage in what people in theological education circles call "exegesis." As noted in Chapter 2, the term simply means "to draw out" by studying a text's history, reading it in the original language if possible (this is why seminaries teach Greek and Hebrew), comparing it with similar stories (for example, when Jesus' parables or sayings appear in two or more of the four gospels), and discovering how interpreters through the centuries have understood its meaning.

As in preparing to proclaim the word so in our anticipation of worship, we make an effort to discern congregational culture. Is worship a highly structured, formal affair that invariably follows a prescribed liturgical order? Have former ministers preached from the pulpit with carefully crafted sermons that were later published for broader distribution? Or is this congregation's ethos one of informality and spontaneity where members design creative liturgies, where no two Sundays unfold in the same way, and where interruptions are expected, including oral feedback to the preacher as she or he preaches? Does the congregation see itself as "church" apart from

> **All churches are "liturgical":** Churches are often lumped into the broad categories of "liturgical" and "non-liturgical." Our English word liturgy comes from Greek antecedents that mean simply "the work of the people." Inasmuch as every Christian community conducts its "work of worship" in some order, all churches have their own particular liturgy. This recognition may help overcome barriers to greater ecumenical breakthroughs, thereby better honoring Jesus' fervent prayer in John 17:11, "that they may be one."

other faith communities in the local area and its own denomination (for those that are not independent, often called "community" churches), or is there a high level of connectedness in which "our church" is viewed as but one outpost or local expression of a diocese, synod, or presbytery and of a national church body and global communion? Only when we understand a community, speak its language, and know its people on a deep level can we stand in its midst as an agent of grace.

## Leading Worship: A Holy Privilege

In our calls to serve at seminaries for many years, we have had multiple opportunities to participate in gatherings of alumni who return to campus after a few or many years since their graduations. At some of these events—for example, when awards or tributes are conferred upon ministers deemed distinguished by their peers and seminary officials—the graduates are invited to reflect upon their careers. Seminary officials, of course, hope the honorees will say laudatory things about the school that prepared them so well for their outstanding work! Almost invariably at such occasions, one hears those being granted recognition speak of a sense of privilege in being called to lead a community (or, over the course of a career, several communities in many cases) of God's faithful people. Most speakers point to the opportunity to lead public worship as among the particular joys experienced in ministry.

Pointing to the centrality of worship in the life of the Christian community, Eugene Peterson writes in his commentary on Revelation 15, "Worship is the essential and central act of the Christian. We do many other things in preparation for and as a result of worship: sing, write, witness, heal, teach, paint, serve, help, build, clean, smile. But the centering act is worship. . . . When we worship it doesn't look like we are doing much—and we aren't. We are looking at what God is doing and orienting our action to the compass points of creation and covenant, judgment and salvation."[1]

While Sundays roll around very quickly, especially for those in their early years of public ministry, and sometimes may cause a degree of weariness by their unrelenting regularity, most clergy and other ministers look forward to the weekly (or in some traditions more frequent) gathering of the faithful in communal worship. If the most important hour of the week for a parish community is to be a high-quality experience—a holy time in which worshippers truly feel God's presence in unique ways that are otherwise not felt—careful preparation on the part of leaders is required. While spontaneity has its place (remember Philip's response in Acts 8:26-40, when the Ethiopian eunuch pleaded for baptism on the spot?), worship planning far in advance of a given service is often required. Selecting and arranging music and scheduling readers, ushers, altar guild workers, assisting ministers, and others may require weeks or months of preparation and planning. Many churches plan seasonally in order that, for example, the Lenten period finds worship centered about a theme with a continuous series of Scripture readings or homilies on the Lord's Prayer, creeds, or other key doctrines or central elements of the faith.

Many churches follow a lectionary, a prescribed cycle of readings. The three-year Revised Common Lectionary has been widely adopted ecumenically to guide Scripture readings in line with the liturgical calendar. This calendar revolves around the two major feasts of the Christian year—Christmas and Easter, with the corresponding preparatory seasons of Advent (which literally means "coming" of Christ) and Lent (which corresponds to the lengthening of days in springtime and is a season for reflection on the life, death, and passion of Jesus, leading up to the resurrection). Two more seasons follow Christmastide (the twelve days of Christmas) and

Eastertide (the fifty days of Easter), respectively: the season of Epiphany, in which we celebrate the shining of the light of Christ in the world, and the season of Pentecost, in which the gift of the Holy Spirit gives continued growth to the whole Christian community. Churches observing these seasons redecorate the sanctuary according to the colors of these seasons: white for Christmas and Easter, the color of major feasts; blue or purple for Advent and purple and/or sackcloth and dark red for Lent as colors of expectation, penitence, and also royalty; and green for the "growing seasons" of Epiphany and Pentecost. Special feast days are separately marked by white (or white and gold "festal" colors) or by red (for martyrs of the

> **Who tells us what scriptures to read in worship?** Following a three-year cycle, the Revised Common Lectionary (RCL) was developed in the early 1990's by a broad ecumenical group of North American scholars (representing about 20 denominations) who worked together over several years. For each Sunday, readings include passages from the Hebrew Bible (the "Old Testament"), a Psalm, typically a New Testament epistle excerpt, and a portion from one of the four gospels. Decisions about what texts to include were informed by the desire that worshipping communities would be exposed to the breadth of Holy Scripture, with particular focus on texts that proclaim the centrality of Jesus Christ.

church and for the Holy Spirit). The dedicated church members whose job it is to decorate the sanctuary and tend the Communion table, who are sometimes called an altar guild, are kept busy with their special spiritual devotion of changing and caring for the banners, flowers, candles, Communion vessels, and other sacred objects that adorn the worship of each unique place with its particular beauty and reverence.

Those preparing to become public ministers will be given helpful guidance in their formation for the worship leadership dimensions of their calling through seminary liturgy courses and textbooks. Beyond what can be offered in a classroom or online setting, candidates for ministry should be encouraged to seek out a wide variety of worship experiences during their formative period. By observing a broad spectrum of different worship styles and the manifold ways in which ministers exercise their roles as agents of grace, one will be able to form one's own approach to leading a community in its central activity. Most seminary curricula also include a heavy dosage of field education (sometimes called contextual learning) in a parish setting, where a student minister can experiment in leading worship under the mentorship of an experienced practitioner.

How one views the role of worship in a community will shape one's approach to leading the people in their dance with the Divine. Worship can be described as a divine drama in which the people of God are (re-) enactors who recreate some portion of the biblical story and act out how we imagine God would have us relate to one another and to the whole world. There is an overlap, going back to ancient times, between religious ritual and theatrical drama; the earliest plays in Europe were "miracle plays" depicting Christmas and Easter dramas. In many traditions, those who lead worship in a sanctuary "dress up," as do actors performing in a theater. However, liturgy is *not* a performance for an audience. It is a ritual reenactment of sacred stories, songs, and acts of praise and remembrance, in which all those who are gathered are equally participants, and God is both director and audience. Liturgical vestments (albs, cassocks and surplices, stoles, chasubles) signal to the gathered community that "Those people are our leaders—our stewards of the mysteries—who will guide us as we are about our holy work." But even such garments grow out of a communal assumption: the alb and the surplice are both versions of the ancient baptismal garment in which many Christians are still robed before or after their baptisms today—and as such, might appropriately be worn by all the baptized!

In some instances, the worship leaders are cast in the role of leading actress or actor. This tends to be the case when a minister presides at the sacraments or preaches from the pulpit. But often the leader's role is more akin to the producer who works behind the scenes, convening the right group of players, coaching and coaxing them to give their best in God-play.

Holy work is indeed another good image by which to describe the activity of the people of God at worship. The very word *liturgy* is from the Greek *leitourgia*, which translates straightforwardly as "the work of (all) the people." God's people come together to work, to do a job, and among other things, that job is to remind ourselves and others that God is in charge of the world, that God cares for and loves the whole creation, and that God is especially concerned about those the world tends to forget—the poor and marginalized, the oppressed, and those who suffer. Within this framework, those who lead the people at worship are among the workers. We roll up our sleeves, take up the tools of our trade (Bible and songbooks; vessels that contain water, bread, wine, and perhaps also oil or incense; technology to enhance our communication), and go to work.

Still another metaphor for worship is offered by liturgical theologian Gordon Lathrop when he declares, "Christianity is not just an idea or a list of convictions. It is not primarily a religious inclination that an individual might have or a technique to equip an individual to engage with spiritual realities. It is certainly best understood not as a consumer good that an individual might or might not choose to buy in the marketplace of religious ideas. . . . Rather, quite concretely, quite *physically*, Christianity is a *meeting*!"[2] To Lathrop's description of Christianity as meeting (which he goes on to develop further as meeting centered around the meal of Holy Communion), we would add that, beyond their intrinsic value of praise and adoration, gatherings for worship are organizing or staging meetings that launch and sustain mission movements. While the hours at table with the risen Christ were undoubtedly unparalleled in their emotional intensity, the two Emmaus road co-travelers with Jesus must have been startled when he suddenly disappeared from their midst. But they did not linger long at the table in their reverie. Rather, they rushed back to Jerusalem to tell others, who in turn told others. Before long, the good news was spreading like wildfire. In other words, the holy meeting with Jesus in Emmaus was both sacramental meal and mission movement rally. We will delve more deeply into the matter of how mission is conceived in various traditions in today's multifaith global community in subsequent chapters.

With an eye particularly to the missionary dimensions of worship, among other self-conceptions that may be helpful for a public worship leader is the role of translator. This becomes increasingly important in our current context, where more and more people who may dip their toes in the waters of a worship experience come with little or no background in the "church world." We who embrace callings to public ministry tend to be relatively longtime "church types" well versed in the language and familiar with the geography of church world. We do well to remind ourselves often just how alien an experience it is for first-time visitors to walk into a church on a Sunday morning. They are handed a bulletin ("What's this? Do I have to pay for it like a program in a theater?"), ushered (or not) to a hard pew ("Why don't they just call it a bench? At least I don't have to worry about falling asleep on that straight-backed hard thing!"), and surrounded by strangers ("Why are these people so doggone dressed up? Nobody wears suits and ties where I work anymore, and I sure feel out of place here"). And then the service begins. Out walks a person dressed in a white robe ("Hmm . . . that's kind of scary, almost like a cult!"), who makes a bunch of announcements ("She's repeating what I just read in this program; don't they think I can read?") and then turns her back on the crowd to face a wall and starts talking to God ("That seems kind of rude"). Soon others in the crowd pick up a book and begin to sing music like nothing our visitor has ever before encountered ("These folks live in some other age and certainly don't get it when it comes to real music! Oh, and by the way, how the heck am I supposed to know which book to use when there are three in the back of the bench ahead of me?"). Soon the guy or gal in the robe climbs into a walled-in pedestal and begins to use strange and unfamiliar words like *kyrie, grace, salvation, redemption, sacraments,* and *eschatology* ("What's the matter, can't they just talk regular English, or do they think I need to be impressed by their eloquence? Sheesh! I'm sure never coming back here again!").

The reader will grasp the point of the previous paragraph. Though the effort may feel burdensome and interruptive, a faith community that is serious about welcoming strangers will give concerted attention to the work of translation, of keeping it as simple as possible in terms of language, and of frequently explaining—either orally or by means of prominently displayed printed pieces—nomenclature and terminology unique to church world. Such attention to translating into the language of the people was at the heart of the so-called Protestant Reformation, when Martin Luther and others rendered Scripture into German, English, French, and many other languages and changed worship from ancient Latin, which few if any parishioners understood. No less a reformation is required today in many places where growing numbers of would-be churchgoers are simply unaccustomed to our language, liturgies, and general ways of being in ecclesiastical arenas.

An added dimension of this work of translation, which has appropriately gained widespread attention—and caused a fair amount of controversy—during the decades we two have been in ministry, is the whole matter of "inclusive language. The churches in which we both serve, and many others, have issued helpful guidelines for congregations and those who lead them to make the language of worship more accessible to all current and prospective attendees. Pooh-poohed by some, mocked by others, and declared downright heretical by still a few more who resist the introduction of new biblical translations, innovative liturgies, and other gender- and

> The movement to use **"inclusive" or "expansive" language** in worship arose in the 1970's out of concern that the exclusive use of masculine imagery for God and persons reinforced a parallel exclusion of women from leadership in the church—and by extension, the implicit message that men are made more in the image of God than women. From this movement came a further effort by many to increase the expansiveness of language for God and persons to embrace the diversity of the whole Body of Christ, including race, culture, sexual orientation, ability/disability, and other ways in which differences might be celebrated and reflected in our language to describe God and humanity. This extends beyond simply exchanging pronouns, to discovering fresh new metaphors for the divine, as well as recovering under-utilized ancient biblical imagery.

intercultural-enhancing measures, the effort to increase diversity in expression is an area in which we ministers must courageously persist.

If constant reference to God only as "father" keeps out of the Christian community a woman sexually abused by her biological father, then we must find a way to change our language without abandoning altogether the classical Trinitarian description of God as Father, Son, and Holy Spirit. If constant reference to the clergy as "he" (and in some traditions using the title Father for the resident reverend) sends girls and women of all ages the message "This calling isn't for you," we who serve in churches that embrace for ordination both genders must clean up our language. As the internationally renowned Roman Catholic biblical scholar Ronald D. Witherup has written:

> Inclusive language is not a passing fancy of some unreasonable radicals out to destroy the Church. Inclusive language is and will be for the future a necessity in society and the Church. As we have seen in many instances of proper biblical translation, the sense of the biblical and liturgical texts virtually requires attention to inclusive language in instances where the entire

people of God, regardless of sex, are addressed. We can no longer allow our longstanding cultural prejudices to predetermine the way we wrestle with our patriarchal past.[3]

Further, as language for God is always imperfect, built upon limited human experiences of the Divine (as the Jewish tradition of writing the name *God* as "G-d" signifies), so all names for God are imperfect, partial, and metaphorical rather than literal.[4] Some today use the term *expansive language* to signal that traditional language for the Holy need not be eradicated, but should be supplemented with new (and indeed, alternative ancient) forms, in order to create a space for *all* persons' experiences and imaginative renderings of the Divine as S/He continues to move among us. Similarly, visual images that represent Jesus as a blond Scandinavian or God as a white European patriarch should give us pause. Such images divinize whiteness at the expense of the majority of the world's people. The human imagination is a sacred space that can make "plenty good room"[5] for both traditional and expansive words and images for the God of all creation.

The quest for inclusiveness goes beyond mere revision (which in many cases, as Witherup explains, renders more accurate translations) of existing texts and liturgies. Expanding the imagery for God and God's people is another means of enabling more spiritual seekers to find their way into a welcoming community. Retired liturgy and worship professor Marjorie Procter-Smith helps us see that "[t]he interpretive and imaginative nature of the liturgy can be opened up and transformed by the use of feminist liturgical imagination, which takes seriously women's experience and recognizes its legitimacy as religious experience."[6] Similar opportunities exist to help all God's people expand their understandings by incorporating diverse cultural and artistic expressions into a community's worship life.

These are all, in the final analysis, matters of hospitality, one of the most central values of the Christian life, and a guiding principle of both worship and "fellowship" (a churchy word for cultivating friendship in the faith community). In ancient times, hospitality to a stranger was a matter of life and death. Those left out in the cold at night were easy prey for weather, as well as animal and human predators. In the story of the Emmaus road, the disciples urged the risen Jesus to be their guest as the sun went down; he in turn became their host at the table where their eyes were opened in a Eucharistic feast.

## Public Ministers in Multiple Arenas

Thus far, we have focused primarily on the minister as a public servant in the gathered worshipping community. Our remarks could be understood to refer primarily to regular weekly (mostly Sunday) services. Of course, the practice of liturgical leadership involves all the "special services" that include pastoral acts like weddings, funerals or "homegoings," *quinceañeras*, house blessings, prayer breakfasts, offering invocations or benedictions in familial gatherings, graduation ceremonies, openings of legislative sessions, and significant civic events. We get asked to bless all kinds of things from pets to church bells to sporting events. (A famous British photo shows an Anglican priest blessing a pack of hunting hounds and in turn receiving a canine liquid blessing on his shoes!)[7] These occasions can range from deep solemnity to the "holy hilarity" known to the ancient mystics, and sometimes a little of both. Then too, inasmuch as one is always a minister as person, even when not engaged in explicitly ministerial functions, there are countless opportunities to touch others with a word of hope, encouragement, support, and sometimes simple silent presence.

A steward is one who represents and exercises agency on behalf of another or a corporate body. An effective public minister is a connector, a broker, one who bears news and helps make incarnate in the lives of individuals and the gathered people God's very presence and power. This dimension of our calling is both an extraordinary privilege and awesome responsibility! As William H. Willimon concludes his book on the ministry of the ordained, *Calling and Character*, "It is a great blessing to have one's little life caught up in the great doxological crescendo named church, the song sung by the saints throughout the ages, so that we might sing it too today."[8]

## Into the Holy of Holies: Presiding or Assisting at the Sacraments

In the Hebrew Bible (the "Old Testament"), only the high priest was granted the privilege once a year of entering into the "holy of holies" where the ark of the covenant represented the presence of God (Leviticus 16). The writer of Hebrews describes Jesus as "high priest of the good things that have come" (Lev. 9:11) and declares him "the mediator of a new covenant, so that those who are called may receive the promised eternal inheritance"

(9:15). For Christians, the new covenant or contract between God and God's people includes regular reenactment of two key scenes from the life of Jesus. As Jesus was baptized by John the Baptist in the River Jordan, when God's spirit descended upon him in the form of a dove, so Christians are to be baptized by water and the power of the Holy Spirit. And as Jesus concluded his Last Supper with his disciples, his mandate to "do this in remembrance of me" (Luke 22:19) calls for the church in every age to reenact his table fellowship.

These two reenactments (baptism and Holy Communion or Eucharist) are regarded by most Christian traditions, therefore, as sacraments. A sacrament, traditionally defined, is an "outward and visible sign of an inward and spiritual grace, given by Christ as a sure and certain means by which we receive that grace."[9] The late theologian Marianne Micks used the metaphor of a magnifying glass to explain how sacraments "work": grace is all around us at all times, like the diffuse light of the sun; the sacraments focus the light in a particular place so that its effect is more visibly active, the way a magnifying glass focuses sunlight and can even start a fire.[10] Perhaps the best understanding is that these are gifts from God that help us to know and experience God's presence in our lives more deeply. The Greek word for these is mysteries (*mysterion*), not because they are shrouded in secrecy, but because as God's gift, they go beyond or transcend our human powers of complete comprehension. They are not acts of magic that manipulate or change God, but rather, they change us. Baptism is the rite of initiation into Christian community by which we are "justified"—freed from the burden of sin and death—and Communion brings us together with Christ and one another as a sign of our ongoing growth in holiness ("sanctification"), empowering us for mission and giving us strength for the journey. These specific sacraments, in turn, may help us see even more clearly how all of life is sacramental, as we can notice and experience more fully the grace of God poured into our lives in the ordinary moments of daily life.

Within the broad Christian family, there are, of course, a variety of understandings and practices regarding the sacraments per se. In many cases, what we in North America call denominations have resulted from disputes over the sacraments. Such disagreements include matters like who should be baptized and at what stage of life (infants and small children or only adults who can make a personal profession of faith prior to baptism); whether the bread and wine of Holy Communion actually become the body and blood of Christ (*transubstantiation*), are elements conveying the "real presence" of Christ but with the substances of bread and wine remaining unchanged, or are a memorial meal following Christ's commandment; and who may preside at the sacraments (only clergy ordained by a bishop or those whose ordination is by a local congregation). Of lesser consequence, and therefore typically not church-dividing the way the previously mentioned issues have been, are matters like how Communion is distributed (with communicants coming up front to stand or kneel in small groups, or remaining in their pews, where all partake at the same moment), whether wine or grape juice is offered, and the frequency of its celebration (in a growing number of traditions, weekly has become the norm in recent decades, while others feel the holy meal, like a family banquet, retains a more special nature by being engaged in only a few times per year).

While it has been gratifying over the course of our lifetimes to witness and participate in a growing rapprochement among Christian churches (denominations), differences remain and are likely to do so for quite some time as the ecumenical movement inches along in dialogues about the ongoing controversial areas. Regardless of these continuing differing sacramentologies, however, it is probably safe to say that in almost every Christian tradition, "the ministers" play a key role when the community collectively enters the "holy of holies" in sacramental celebrations. Even in denominations with a broad understanding of "minister" to mean every baptized Christian (as in the Lutheran vision of the priesthood of all believers), presiding at worship services during which the sacraments are reenacted is generally reserved for one who is ordained or set apart for a public ministry leadership role. In recognition of the sacred nature of what occurs when a community enters into the "holy of holies," therefore, both presiding and assisting ministers who lead the people in sacramental moments should exercise great care and maintain a spirit of reverence in conducting meetings of the faithful in which the sacraments stand at the center.

We all probably have our own internal images of what a holy demeanor looks like. Pause for a moment and let your mind's eye envision the dress and demeanor of the high priest on his (sadly, there were no women in the ranks back then!) annual entry into the holy of holies. Do you see a bedraggled, unshaven, half-hungover priest bumbling his way into the small cubicle where the very *Shekinah* (a Hebrew word meaning "God's manifested glory") was believed to reside? For those who have a diametrically opposed view to such an image, everyone who presides in worship should under all circumstances be dressed primly and properly in finely pressed liturgical vestments topped by a clerical collar. For others, more casual dress is deemed entirely appropriate in worship, including when the sacraments are celebrated. Some believe that an "overdressed" worship leader can be a deterrent for evangelism, turning off spiritual seekers who come to church desperately seeking acceptance just as they are, torn jeans and tattered T-shirt included. As noted at the outset of this chapter, context is critical in this regard as well. A military chaplain presiding at Holy Communion from the hood of a battlefield vehicle may form an inviting target if she or he stands there in bright liturgical garb with arms uplifted! In relaxed settings like a church camp or retreat center, those who preside at a baptism or service of Holy Communion may make the gathered community most comfortable by choosing more casual dress than worn in the more formal worship space back home. As a bare minimum, however, those who enter the holy of holies should give thoughtful, careful attention to their dress and demeanor, recognizing we do represent Jesus in the reenactment of the Holy Supper and we do carry out Jesus' mission mandate when we obey his command to "go and baptize."

Before going further to expand a bit on the public minister's role in sacramental leadership at baptisms and Holy Communion, it needs to be acknowledged that here we come to a major fork in the road. We need to acknowledge two main branches within Christianity (some would say "camps," but that sounds too militaristic and contentious to those of us who remain hopeful that, slowly but surely, the branches are becoming more intertwined and may eventually form a single solid trunk). Those readers from more broadly "Catholic" or "liturgical" traditions (among others, Orthodox, Roman Catholic, and some Anglicans/Episcopalians) may be protesting, "But there are seven sacraments, not just two!" Others from the more "Protestant" side of the Christian family acknowledge the vital importance and centrality in Christian life of marriage, confirmation, penance and reconciliation (forgiveness of sins), anointing of the sick (including but not limited to extreme unction or last rites for the dying), and holy orders or ordination, but view these as sacramental rites or pastoral acts, rather than sacraments. A primary rationale for limiting the sacraments to just two is that whereas all Christians are baptized and encouraged to frequent Holy Communion, following Jesus' exhortation, not all need be confirmed, married, ordained, or anointed. And with regard to the classic Anglican adage about private confession, "None must, all may, some should."[11] Nevertheless, whether these five "lesser sacraments" are considered full sacraments or sacramental rites, they are all solemn occasions that mark significant mileposts in many Christians' journeys of faith.

## Baptismal Ministry: Gift and Challenge

We have acknowledged already the two broad groups within Christianity when it comes to *who* should be baptized (all persons, including those too young to profess their faith, versus believers who can personally attest to their faith prior to being baptized). The other bifurcation within the Christian family is based upon two different views as to how it is done—either by sprinkling or pouring water over the head of a baptisand at a font (a basin or small fountain, often placed on a pedestal near the front of the church or the entrance door as a reminder of members' baptisms) or else by full immersion in a river, lake, or large tank of water in a congregation's regular place of worship. While both traditions largely agree on the benefits of baptism—entry into the church, forgiveness of sins, empowerment for faithful Christian living, and being baptized into the death and resurrection of Jesus Christ (Rom. 6:3)—the differing approaches to the sacrament itself will shape how ministers performing baptisms prepare for and conduct the liturgy.

Here, near the beginning of the twenty-first century, there are probably few areas of public ministry that cause more consternation for some colleagues than baptism. Most of us who have some years of experience can tell tales of challenging and even bizarre requests to "just get it done, and when I/we want it!" One of us (Michael) was approached five minutes before a Christmas Eve worship with a request to baptize the baby of first-time visitors. When queried a bit, they acknowledged they were Roman Catholics who had not discussed with their local priest this idea of having their child baptized in a Lutheran parish. While it has not happened for either of us, many colleagues share stories of being asked amid tears and anguish to baptize a stillborn baby or a person who died in the emergency room without having been baptized. Preparing for baptismal ministry requires thinking through in advance such scenarios and how one will ultimately respond in each unique situation, including both liturgical and pastoral theological reflection.

As ministers who steward the sacramental mysteries, we strive for a balance between providing a pastoral response to individuals and maintaining the integrity of our particular church's teachings about baptism. If our perceptions are correct, the general tide within Christianity in recent decades has been moving away from private baptism in homes or a sanctuary where only a handful of the baptisand's family and friends may gather. A growing cadre of Christians seem to agree with the understanding of baptism articulated by our colleague Kirsi Stjerna, who claims, "As a spiritual sign and a starting point for spiritual living, baptism is tied essentially to the life of the church, the spiritual home where baptism is celebrated and taught with history and shared faith behind. Baptism's benefits are personal, but it is also a public act and one of the essential signs and gifts of the church and its ministry in the world."[12] If baptism inaugurates a person into the church, then it makes sense that *the church* (not just a few members) be present in a regular public service of worship. Undoubtedly, there will be occasions when a private or emergency baptism is called for—the likely-to-die scenario in a hospital already noted or a situation where a fragile infant's delicate health may be compromised by taking her or him into a public setting. But baptism is never truly an emergency, although some churches make provision for "emergency baptism." We can assure people that a loving God would never reject or condemn a child or other person who dies without the benefit of the sacrament. If sacraments are finally God's gift, and God's grace is truly abounding everywhere, then in the words of Paul, "neither death, nor life, nor angels, nor rulers, nor things present, nor things to come, nor powers, nor height, nor depth, nor anything else in all creation, will be able to separate us from the love of God in Christ Jesus our Lord" (Rom. 8:38-39).

Regardless of the pastoral decision rendered regarding place, time, and community participation in a baptism, careful preparation of the baptisands and their supporting families and sponsors is crucial. While a graduate course on the finer points of baptismal theology is probably not appropriate for candidates for baptism or their parents or sponsors, teaching the basics of what it means, how one can fulfill the promises made, and how those who surround the newly baptized can support her or him in the fledgling life of faith should be core components of pre-baptismal classes or individual conferences or counseling.

The conduct of a baptism itself may seem rather straightforward. At a certain point in the service, the presiding ministers invite the baptisand(s) and sponsors (or "godparents") to come forward. The liturgy itself likely will be printed in the bulletin or available in the worship book. Depending on where a congregation is in its liturgical growth and development, it may or may not be necessary to remind folks of the participatory nature of the baptismal liturgy. In addition to the core elements of pouring water or immersing while uttering the appropriate baptismal pronouncement, baptism often include a variety of other symbols, like a candle, chrism oil, and the presentation of a certificate verifying the baptism and noting its date, locale, and those involved in the ceremony. Hasty last-minute preparations—misspelled names or other incorrect information on a certificate, for example—may convey a lackadaisical attitude unbefitting the dignity and holiness of

---

**The Importance of Remembering Our Baptisms:** When tempted or depressed, Martin Luther was wont to exclaim, "But I am baptized!" Some churches have formal liturgies whereby believers recall their baptisms. Similarly, in some congregations the font, always filled with water, is at the entrance to the worship space and members are encouraged to dip their fingers in the water and cross themselves to recall their baptismal status. Some congregations even send baptismal birthday cards or in Sunday worship pray for all those with baptismal anniversaries that week.

---

the occasion. So as stated previously regarding all worship preparedness, giving careful attention to detail well ahead of the occasion will serve all involved, and is part and parcel of the presiding minister's responsibility.

## Holy Communion: Cultivating a Gracious Altar-Side Manner

We probably have all heard the expression *bedside manner* in describing a physician or other health practitioner. It has long been recognized that, in addition to in-depth knowledge and the ability to apply such expertise, a good doctor needs strong relational abilities that signal her or his care for a patient. Similarly, the people of God will be enabled to worship "in spirit and truth" (John 4:24) as they have confidence in the "altar-side" manner of those who are presiding and assisting. Seminary worship classes will help prepare aspiring ministers who will preside or assist at Holy Communion. By paying close attention to your liturgy professors, observing a broad range of practitioners at their altars, and actually practicing at an altar in a pretend service of Communion, you can begin to get comfortable in the mechanics of multitasking required as you handle the elements, read liturgical texts, and coordinate the activity of others involved in a Eucharistic celebration. Yet, say many veterans who recall their early years in ministry, there is more involved than just mastering the manual acts (what to do with your hands and when) and celebrant's role. The most important dimension of becoming a gracious presider or assisting minister is cultivating a presence that is at once confidence inspiring and welcoming, simultaneously reverent and relaxed, signaling to the gathered community that a loving, forgiving, justice-restoring God is about to show up.

Among the texts used widely in seminary worship courses, now nearly four decades after it was first published and more than twenty years after the author died, is Robert Hovda's *Strong, Loving and Wise*. In this short classic in the field of liturgy, Hovda captures the essence of what is required of and that which should be avoided by every minister who stands before the people of God and cohosts the holy meal with the risen Christ:

> In the liturgical assembly we are striving to be at the height of our God-consciousness, and therefore of our human-consciousness. It is an awesome thing to face the mystery of the Other and the mystery of ourselves with such purpose and intent. It is intolerable that such an assembly should be led by a person who has no apparent interest in the proceedings, or by a person who seems to be using the situation to dominate, or to display, or to collect the plaudits of a crowd.[13]

Hovda's description of a strong, loving, and wise presider or assistant calls for striking the right balance between reverent seriousness and lightheartedness at the altar. One should strive for a hospitable demeanor that welcomes all to the banquet table, without either being overly folksy or coming across like an uptight drill sergeant who barks orders at subordinates trembling in their albs. On some occasions, we need to be self-forgiving, for inevitably we will make mistakes, lose our place in the liturgy, get tongue-tied, or even make more serious gaffes like dropping the bread or a chalice full of wine!

Since those who lead the Communion liturgy do "stand in for Jesus" at the holy meal, there is a sense in which presiders and assistants are sacred actors, in some traditions even understood as vessels or channels of God's

---

**Communion is a meal:** The sacrament of the altar goes by several names (for example, "Holy Communion," "The Lord's Supper," "Holy Eucharist"). References to the Lord's Supper or the Last Supper remind communicants that Holy Communion really is a meal! In the early church, it was celebrated as a full sit-down dinner (Acts 2:46b), and it still evokes the unity of the church in breaking bread together and with the risen Christ. Many persons feel that reality is further reinforced by using actual bread rather than pre-fabricated wafers, and congregants baking bread for the holy table can be a reverent shared form of ministry.

---

grace. Like good performers on other stages, we can give attention to cultivating our voices, being adequately amplified or projecting so that all may hear the liberating and life-giving words that transform ordinary elements into the "bread of heaven" and "cup of salvation."[14] We must be actors with authenticity whose presence at the altar exudes a genuine piety—the belief that our words and actions are not fiction but that the story we reenact is true. Although the sacraments depend on God's action, not our own, to be efficacious (to do the work of offering God's grace), our reverence both shares and models the sincerity of heart with which all believers should approach the sacraments. As viewed by others who look to the activity at the altar, the person of the minister cannot be entirely separated from all she or he represents—and that includes in some measure Jesus. When we stand altar-side, we are agents, representatives, ambassadors of the risen Christ. But we need not be perfect! Dorothy McRae-McMahon, minister of Pitt Street Uniting Church in Sydney, Australia, wrote these reassuring words:

> In our hands lie the bread and the wine and the water of the grace of baptism. When these precious elements were placed in my hands on the day of my ordination, I wondered if I would ever be worthy of carrying them. But as I broke the bread and offered the wine, I realized that the life I held would never be dependent on me or the strength or worthiness of my hands.

A presence was always there in once-offered grace and freedom; it was simply named by me and claimed in thanksgiving by the people of God."[15]

Above all, with all our human frailties, we are called in humility to be "stewards of the mysteries of God" (1 Cor. 4:1).

 ## Questions for Personal Exploration

1. As you contemplate entering the "holy of holies" as a worship leader, what excites you, and what causes anxiety?
2. From your own experiences or observation of others, what are some practices that create space for authentic worship, and what practices, attitudes, or actions detract from our experience of the holy?
3. As you imagine what "holy demeanor" looks like, what in your demeanor might need to change in order to cultivate a gracious altar-side manner?
4. Many congregations experience distressing "worship wars" or "altar-cations." What are some possible ways of avoiding such tensions or resolving such conflicts?
5. Just as it is foolish for a doctor to be her own physician, or unwise for a lawyer to act as his own attorney, so ministers may be unable to be "stewards of the mysteries" for themselves and their families. If such is the case, how might you seek opportunities to be at prayer and worship without having always to "perform"?
6. Thinking back over your life, what moments would you identify as being sacramental in nature? What was it about them that made them holy or sacred?

 ## Resources for Deeper Exploration

Costen, Melva W. *African American Christian Worship.* 2nd ed. Nashville: Abingdon, 2009.

Dawn, Marva J. *A Royal "Waste" of Time: The Splendor of Worshiping God and Being Church for the World.* Grand Rapids: Eerdmans, 1999.

Long, Kimberly Bracken. *The Worshiping Body: The Art of Leading Worship.* Louisville: Westminster John Knox, 2009.

Senn, Frank. *Introduction to Christian Liturgy.* Minneapolis: Fortress Press, 2012.

*Worship Matters* series. Multiple titles and authors. Minneapolis: Augsburg Fortress, 2005–2014. Details at www.augsburgfortress.org/worshipmatters.

## ◉⊙ Notes

1. Eugene H. Peterson, *Reversed Thunder: The Revelation of John and the Praying Imagination* (New York: HarperCollins, 1988), 140.

2. Gordon Lathrop, *The Pastor: A Spirituality* (Minneapolis: Fortress Press, 2006), 59.

3. Ronald D. Witherup, *A Liturgist's Guide to Inclusive Language* (Collegeville, MN: Liturgical, 1996), 68.

4. On metaphor, see Pamela Cooper-White, *Braided Selves* (Eugene, OR: Cascade, 2011), 1–16.

5. The phrase is the title of a well-known African American spiritual.

6. Marjorie Procter-Smith, *In Her Own Rite: Constructing Feminist Liturgical Tradition* (Nashville: Abingdon, 1990), 56.

7. The photo appears frequently, for example, on the Bridlewood Equestrian Facility's announcement of its First Annual Hunter Derby, 2008, http://www.bridlewoodok.com /HunterDerby.html.

8. William H. Willimon, *Calling & Character: Virtues of the Ordained Life* (Nashville: Abingdon, 2000), 150.

9. *The Book of Common Prayer* (New York: Church Publishing, 1979), 857.

10. Marianne Micks, *Loving the Questions: An Exploration of the Nicene Creed* (New York: Church Publishing, 2004), 86.

11. For example, see Michael Becker, *Confession: None Must, All May, Some Should* (Cincinnati: Forward Movement, 2004).

12. Kirsi Stjerna, *No Greater Jewel: Thinking about Baptism with Luther* (Minneapolis: Augsburg Fortress, 2009), 15.

13. Robert W. Hovda, *Strong, Loving and Wise*, (Collegeville, MN: Liturgical, 1976), 13.

14. *The Book of Common Prayer* (New York: Church Publishing, 1979), 365.

15. Dorothy McRae-McMahon, *Being Clergy, Staying Human: Taking Our Stand in the River* (Washington, DC: Alban Institute, 1992), 72.

# Chapter 4

# Companions in Healing: Practices of Pastoral Care

And he said to them, "What are you discussing with each other while you walk along?" They stood still, looking sad.

—LUKE 24:17A

A long the Emmaus road, says Luke's gospel, Jesus interpreted to his fellow travelers all things that the Scriptures had to say about him. Now, while the gospels had yet to be written, including those portions where Jesus' sayings about himself were recorded, we might imagine his interpreting how various Hebrew Bible texts about shepherds (with the best-known being Psalm 23) pointed to him as the Good Shepherd. The word *pastoral* comes, of course, from *pastor*, which means shepherd. This has been the traditional metaphor or model—the pastoral caregiver as the shepherd. The shepherd tends the flock, feeds and guides the sheep, protects them from wolves and marauders, and generally steers them in the direction they are to go. And drawing on Christ's own words, the shepherd "lays down his life for the sheep" (John 10:11b). This was taken seriously by generations of pastoral caregivers who felt a call to sacrificial love of their flock and the task of moral and spiritual guidance. But herein lies a serious pitfall—the tendency to see self-sacrifice as a defining image of ministry.

While some sacrifice is probably always necessary in a devoted Christian life, the dominance of a sacrificial image has caused numerous problems. In particular, it can lead to taking oneself so seriously that one might view one's own pastoral ministry as so uniquely indispensable that one's

71

own needs as a caregiver can be neglected indefinitely, and if the pastoral caregiver or his or her family should suffer for this, it is all within the framework of the self-sacrificial love of the shepherd. Also, the truth is, who in any congregation wants to be thought of simply as a sheep?!

> **The word *pastor* means shepherd.** This traditional image, associated with Christ, has lately been supplemented by images, such as that of the Good Samaritan discussed later in this chapter, which do not encourage unhealthy self-sacrifice, or over-identification with the Savior. The image of tender care, however, continues to be one of many helpful images of pastoral care.

This paradigm of the pastor as shepherd is now shifting. In large part, this is due to the influence of two very important and interrelated strands of theological thinking and pastoral praxis: the growing presence of women in both lay and ordained leadership in many mainline denominations, and the emergence, in part through liberation theology (see chapter 1), of Two-Thirds World[1] voices in theology and of at least slight growth in diversity of racial and class diversity in U.S. churches. These influences, from their own social locations and theological perspectives, have brought critiques of the Shepherd paradigm. No one, it should be noted, is trying to throw the baby (or the shepherd?) out with the bathwater. But there is an increasing awareness of the limitations of this individualistic, heroic model and a wonderful opening up of possibilities for a much wider horizon for pastoral care and pastoral theological thinking.

This opening or widening process may be seen in at least five aspects of pastoral practice: (1) listening as primary practice; (2) context; (3) content; (4) diversification; and (5) balance.

## Listen, Listen, Listen!

Pastoral care involves learning to trust that silence is truly facilitative. Less is more! A lot of pastoral care simply involves getting out of the way so that the Holy Spirit can do the healing work necessary. We are not to be psychotherapists (or worse, pseudo-therapists!). A good way of explaining the

**Listening is the most important skill in pastoral care.** While many imagine that pastoral care implies giving wise advice, or dispensing theological wisdom, these play a relatively small role in good care and counseling. The best care depends mainly upon showing empathy, helping persons to tell and hear their own stories, and encouraging their own listening for the movement of the Spirit in their lives.

domains of pastoral care, vis-à-vis therapy, is the chart in figure 4.1, called the Johari window.[2]

In this diagram, areas 1 and 3 are the usual domains of pastoral care, involving conscious communication between pastor and pastoral-care recipient. Domain 1 is the social level, where what the parishioner shares is fully conscious (known to self) and easily shared with others. Domain

|  | Known to Self | Not Known to Self |
|---|---|---|
| **Known to Others** | 1<br><br>Social Level<br><br>— Pastoral Care — | 2<br><br>Risk Level<br><br>— Pastoral Care &<br>Counseling — |
| **Not Known to Others** | 3<br><br>Private Life<br>Space<br><br>— Pastoral Care &<br>Counseling — | 4<br><br>Unknown/<br>Unconscious<br><br>— Pastoral<br>Psychotherapy — |

**Figure 4.1** The Johari Window, adapted

Source: Adapted from Vincent D'Andrea and Peter Salovey, *Peer Counseling: Skills and Perspectives* (Palo Alto, CA: Science and Behavior Books, 1983), 63, citing Joseph Luft, *Group Processes: An Introduction to Group Dynamics*, 3rd ed. (New York: McGraw-Hill, 1984).

3 also is fully conscious for the parishioner but involves matters of more privacy and is more carefully boundaried. Issues belonging to domain 3 can be shared when the parishioner feels there is sufficient trust and rapport with the pastoral caregiver. This requires time to develop. The caregiver needs to exercise patience, non-intrusiveness (not being pushy or having an agenda for the parishioner to follow), and devotion to nonjudgmental listening. Domain 2 also is, on occasion, an area for pastoral care; it covers personal feelings and behaviors that the pastor observes in the parishioner (even if the parishioner is not fully aware of them) and on occasion, for the good of the congregation, needs to tactfully confront. This is an area of risk and requires great sensitivity and tact, because exposing to a person what others observe and know about, though the person is unaware, tends to evoke shame. Therefore, while occasionally the domain of pastoral care when gentle confrontation is required,[3] domain 2 is more the purview of pastoral counseling and psychotherapy. The fourth quadrant is the realm of pastoral psychotherapy and not pastoral care. It represents the realm of the unconscious.

### Transference and Countertransference

The foregoing distinctions require a brief explanation of two interlocking dynamics in all helping relationships; these dynamics are called transference and countertransference. Transference is a particular form of projection, in which we (unconsciously) project our internal emotional experiences of other persons—especially from childhood—onto the "screen" of another person and begin to treat that person as if she or he were an earlier figure in our life. For example, if one of my parents was highly critical, I might unconsciously assume that about my boss and react accordingly, even when the facts about my boss suggest otherwise. We all do this. It's a part of our natural psychological development and a strong determinant in the formation of our personalities. It manifests itself in marriage, in friendships, and in work relationships, and as one person's projections interact with another's, it can also be a powerful mutual dynamic in groups, including congregations.[4] Transference, as a subset of projection, is a natural unconscious set of feelings, thoughts, fantasies, and to some extent behaviors that occur whenever we are in the position of being cared for, taught, evaluated, supervised, and/or governed by another person. We unconsciously project or "transfer" the feelings we had as infants and children onto those who have some kind of authority for or over us today. Without realizing it, we are reminded of the feelings we had toward our parents and other early caretakers, on whom we depended initially for our very survival and later for our physical and emotional well-being. The better our experiences of being parented, the easier our relationships to authority in adulthood will also be. However, no one has "perfect" parents, and no one escapes childhood entirely unscathed emotionally.

Extremes of abuse and neglect can cause significant suffering and damage to a person's self-esteem, personal boundaries, and ability to trust. But even more subtle experiences of emotional neglect, rigidity, or judgmentalism can trigger unconscious expectations of those who have some kind of power over us—even in the most benign forms. For this reason, pastoral caregivers are trained to be aware of ways in which we are always on the receiving end of some kind of transference from those for whom we care. While it is only the domain of pastoral psychotherapy (domain 4 in the Johari window) to explore and in some sense rework this transference dynamic, our awareness in all the domains of care and counseling will help us not to get drawn in unwittingly to reenacting unhealthy dramas from the parishioner's past.

Just as transference occurs in the unconscious feelings of a parishioner toward a pastoral caregiver, so caregivers also project our own "stuff"—our own unresolved emotional issues or baggage—onto those in our care. This is traditionally called countertransference in psychotherapy, but a more useful way of thinking about it is how we most helpfully can use ourselves as instruments for understanding the other person, while keeping our own

---

Technical terms **transference and countertransference** are crucial in listening to another without distortion or projection. Classically defined, transference is what parishioners unconsciously imagine about us and possibly act out toward us, based on their earliest childhood relationships. Countertransference is *our* own unconscious imaginings, or *projections*, onto them, based on our own unresolved issues. The better aware we are of our own issues and the better we appreciate that unconscious dynamics are always flowing, the more we can get beyond these to a clearer picture of the real needs of those who turn to us to listen to them and provide care.

getting in the way.[5] Many if not most seminary students will
c only in an introductory pastoral-care course, but also in a hospital-
ımunity-based clinical pastoral education (CPE) program, where the
ortance of self-awareness as a caregiver and ways of understanding our
ʌvn personal history, feelings, and habitual behaviors can be explored in
the direct practice of pastoral care and in small groups of peers receiving the
same training together.

## Pastoral Counseling and Psychotherapy

In the Johari window (figure 4.1), notice that there is a distinction between
pastoral counseling and pastoral psychotherapy. Pastoral psychotherapy, as
previously stated, is the domain in which unconscious dynamics are more
intensively explored through such techniques as free association, dream
interpretation, and exploration of reenactments of childhood thoughts,
fantasies, and emotions as they become evident in the relationship with
the therapist. It is a branch of mental health counseling in which some of
the deepest and most intractable emotional issues can be addressed, and
it may be brief (a period of weeks or months) but is often longer-term,
even two years or more. Pastoral psychotherapists are extensively trained in
both theology and clinical psychology, and are normally both endorsed by
a religious body and certified and/or licensed by a variety of professional
organizations, such as the American Association of Pastoral Counselors,
and state licensing boards. Pastoral counseling is another mode of pastoral
helping that goes beyond short-term and supportive pastoral care, both
in the level of risk and intimacy and in duration. Like psychotherapy, it
belongs in the realm of greater training and specialization of certified and/
or licensed counselors. However, in contrast to pastoral psychotherapy,
Pamela has previously defined pastoral counseling as focusing mainly on
*conscious* emotional and mental processes (or, at most, preconscious—that
is, mental contents that may be temporarily out of awareness but are easily accessible once some attention has been paid).[6] The goal is to help a
client solve problems in his or her present situation, often by identifying
and building on his or her existing strengths. Unlike psychotherapy, which
primarily addresses long-term pathology, trauma, or serious and enduring
patterns of emotional distress, pastoral counseling primarily addresses ways
in which the client can become more self-aware and thoughtful about his
or her behaviors, feelings, and life choices.

Obviously, in practice there is considerable overlap between therapy and counseling. The primary means of healing in pastoral counseling is through a cognitive, or mental, reframing of the client's current situation and the adoption of new strategies for coping, although some focus may be given to antecedents in the client's early life. Pastoral counseling, then—including cognitive, cognitive-behavioral, Solution Focused,[7] Rational-Emotive,[8] and many contemporary narrative approaches[9]—tends to focus on the present and future rather than present and past emotional events, and it works through various methods of reframing of negative perspectives or meanings to events in order to arrive at solutions to problems identified by clients. Much or all of what is discussed in sessions—usually about once a

> **Care, counseling and therapy are not the same!** *Pastoral care* is generally short-term, focused on spiritual support and an assessment-referral model for serious or long-term problems of *parishioners*. Pastoral counseling and pastoral psychotherapy both require further training in clinical psychology beyond seminary. *Pastoral counseling* tends to focus on solving problems and self-defeating patterns of thought and behavior that are troubling the *client*. *Pastoral psychotherapy* tends to focus on unconscious dynamics in both the *patient*'s past and present. All of these modes of helping are pastoral because they acknowledge spirituality as a central aspect of each person's life, and recognize that God/Christ/ the Spirit are involved in the work of healing—and, as well, a central source of support for the pastoral caregiver him/herself.

week—involves events and feelings of the client that have occurred outside the counseling relationship, in the client's experiences with everyday living during the week. The language used to describe the therapeutic dyad in this enterprise is usually (pastoral) "counselor" and "client," giving emphasis to the respectful, contractual nature of the professional relationship.

In real practice, this distinction between counseling and psychotherapy, and even care, is not so pure at times, and there is some overlap. The chief difference is most often seen in the focus of attention in the counseling/therapy session: counseling will focus almost entirely on the client's situation and problems outside the session, while psychotherapy will increasingly focus over time on the interaction between the therapist and the patient in the here-and-now of the therapeutic session, in an effort to "catch" unconscious projective processes "in the act," *in media res* ("in the midst of things") as a mirror for understanding the unconscious processes that are likely also being enacted in the patient's everyday life.

## In Pastoral Care, Less Is More!

Another very important dimension of listening as primary in pastoral care is the issue of advice. Simply stated, giving advice is not our job! There is a lot of truth in the notion that the advice that worked for me may not work for you. I should not project my situation, my feelings, my solutions onto your problems. This is one of the more negative forms of countertransference, especially if I am doing this unwittingly. The best way I can guard against that is by listening to you, as in the popular Buddhist saying "Don't just do something—sit there!"

This is sometimes called ministry of presence. People, young and old and in between, know when someone is really there for them. We may be tempted to feel that we should be doing more, or at least giving reassurance, but we all too often underestimate what the gift of just being there, being with, can mean to folks. Reassurance can be received as both false and toxic! Theologian Nicholas Wolterstorff, in his memoir of grief after the death of his young adult son, offers the metaphor of the mourning bench:

> Please: Don't say it's not really so bad. Because it is. Death is awful, demonic. If you think your task as comforter is to tell me that really, all things considered, it's not so bad, you do not sit with me in my grief but place yourself off in the distance away from me. Over there, you are of no help. What I need to hear from you is that you recognize how painful it is. I need to hear from you that you are with me in my desperation. To comfort me, you have to come close. Come sit beside me on my mourning bench.[10]

Wolterstorff is describing in very personal terms the difference between *sympathy* and *empathy*. Sympathy, or feeling-with, is not all bad! It's a feeling of kindness toward the other person. But sympathy is also felt at arm's length: "You over there are suffering, and I'm sorry that you are. But I over here am just fine." Empathy, in contrast, means feeling-in. While we can never fully know what another person is feeling (and in fact, it is empathic

> **Sympathy vs. Empathy**: *Sympathy* is feeling-with. It can be an
> expression of genuine kindness, but it stands at a distance.
> *Empathy* is feeling-in, stepping into the other person's shoes
> and to the extent possible, trying to understand the other's feelings
> from his or her own point of view. Pastoral care strives for empathy,
> which is healing in itself.

to acknowledge that), empathy happens when we begin to feel what the other person is feeling and experience what she or he is experiencing. To the best of our ability, we walk in the other's shoes. The first and foremost goal of listening is empathy. And empathy is healing in and of itself.[11]

## Context: How We Are Shaped by Where We Live

The second arena in which the discipline of pastoral care has undergone some changes has to do with the increased attention to the importance of social and cultural context. As noted throughout this book, context has become one of the most foundational aspects for consideration in all practices of ministry. In pastoral care in particular, this takes a distinctive form by lifting pastoral assessment beyond merely looking for individual pathology in one who comes for help (although this can be very real and should signal a need for referral to a pastoral counselor or psychotherapist). Contextual sensitivity helps pastoral caregivers recognize that much of what ails a person is not internal to the person alone, but is caused by the economic, racial, and social burdens and pressures surrounding a person's life. Carroll Watkins Ali, a pastoral counselor in Denver, tells this story from her pastoral counseling practice, with a client named "Lemonine":

> Truly, life was Lemonine's presenting problem. There are no
> other diagnoses in the traditional sense. Lemonine was basi-
> cally suffering from being overcome by her own personal life,
> while trying to cope with all the external social realities that
> affected each age group of her family members. In essence,
> each weekly session during our relationship served mainly to
> build Lemonine up enough so that she could go back out to
> face a hostile world for another week. A major issue that came
> up often in our sessions was the racism Lemonine experienced
> in her workplace. In fact, she experienced tremendous stress

related to the dynamics of both racism and sexism in corporate America. The glass ceiling barred heavily against her advancement before she could even get her foot in the door because she was both Black and female. She worried about being the last hired and the first fired as a result of corporate downsizing. This actually occurred twice during the course of our sessions. In retrospect, it now seems that therapy was Lemonine's last effort to find a way to overcome the many problems of her world.[12]

## The Family System

Traditional one-on-one models of pastoral care, based on the medical model of psychiatry as the chief form of mental health care, tended to operate in the arena of the individual psyche. However, many pastoral theologians and professors of pastoral care have been trained in a broader paradigm called family systems theory, which was a liberative approach adopted in the 1950s and '60s to move beyond the individualism widespread in both pastoral care and mental health counseling in general. Family systems looked beyond individual pathology to understand how persons are formed in the

---

 **Family systems theory**: Family systems theory is often used in pastoral care and counseling as a way of recognizing that individuals' problems are never isolated from the pulls and pressures of their entire family of origin.

---

interlocking dynamics and largely unconscious rules, roles, and assumptions about how to live, which are passed on from one generation in a family to the next. Utilizing systems theory from economics, engineering, science, and other social sciences, family systems theorists came to understand that families try to maintain "homeostasis"—that is, at their most basic level of functioning, families try to keep individual members from rocking the boat for fear that the family might fall apart.

Families use a variety of strategies to do this, without the members' conscious awareness. One strategy is triangulation, which occurs when two persons in conflict attempt to pull in a third person to take sides, distract, or otherwise reduce the original tension. Another strategy is scapegoating, or assigning blame or pathology to a particular member so that other members of the family can feel innocent or whole. Family members may also divide tasks into rigid roles—for example, the perpetual caretaker, clown, star, or mess-up. Helping any individual in the family to recognize these dynamics can help the whole family, because as one member of a system changes, the rest of the system will tilt and have to find a new (and hopefully healthier) homeostasis.

### The Cultural Context and Issues of Justice

Neither an individualistic nor a family systems approach, while very helpful, can fully address some of the larger dimensions and challenges of human experience, including the social, political, economic, racial, ethnic, and cultural surroundings in which any individual's life is embedded, which

> Pastoral care also attends to **cultural and social context**! Individuals and families do not experience their lives apart from the larger social, political, economic, and cultural contexts in which they live. Carter's and McGoldrick's chart (next page) illustrates the many levels of stress that impact persons and families.

bring additional pressures, stresses, and traumas both acute and ongoing to bear on an individual's growth and the living of a life. In a helpful chart (Fig. 4.2), family theorists Betty Carter and Monica McGoldrick show how external stressors affect not only individuals and immediate families, but also extended families, communities, and entire societies in a combination of both "vertical stressors" (challenges that tend to be permanent or long-enduring) and "horizontal stressors" (challenges that occur at points in time that become life-changing for individuals and groups).[13]

The increasing awareness of these contextual realities has led pastoral theology into an awareness of the connection between pastoral care and the work for justice. In the words of Larry Kent Graham, professor emeritus of Iliff School of Theology in Denver, there has been a shift from "relational humanness" (not bad in itself) to "relational justice."[14] This means that pastoral care can no longer focus on the individual in isolation from the wider context. This takes us into the arena of advocacy as well as individual care, and toward

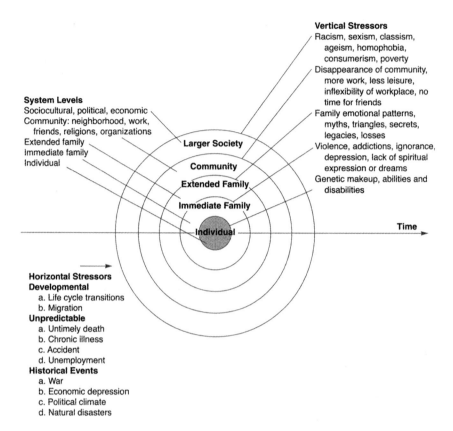

**Figure 4.2** Carter's and McGoldrick's Flow of Stress through the Family

Source: Betty Carter, Monica McGoldrick, and Nydia Garcia-Preto, *The Expanded Family Life Cycle*, 4th ed. (Needham Heights, MA: Allyn & Bacon, 2010), 6.

an awareness that our own openness to the reality and the wisdom of those for whom we care can model mutuality and replace the kind of top-down, power-over expert role that once held sway. We are no longer just called to be good active listeners (listeners who speak mainly to gain better understanding and mirror back what they hear), although that never is a bad idea, but we are also called to hold in our awareness the wider contextual realities in which individuals struggle to live. Similarly, we seek to refrain from diagnosing as individual psychological or spiritual problems what are, in fact, outcomes of societal rather than individual illness and spiritual malaise.

In concrete terms, this means that the arena of care is broadened. No longer confined only to the pastoral caregiver's study, pastoral care may include preaching that calls for empowerment and liberation of persons; offering small groups for support, Bible study, and discipleship aimed toward changing realities that stifle and oppress individuals' lives in the community; and getting out in the wider community, doing "public theology," that is, joining together with others who are working for social change that undergirds the possibility for personal change. To use an example from Pamela's specialized ministry with battered women for many years, it would mean the difference between counseling an individual battered woman about how to take responsibility for changing her life versus taking the broader approach of empowering her to identify her own strengths and options while also preaching, teaching, working collaboratively with battered women's shelters and agencies for men who batter, and advocating with others in the community for the eradication of violence against women and the social structures that reinforce it.

The traditional functions of pastoral care reflected a somewhat more individualistic and even perhaps clergy-centered approach. A kind of subliminal model of the learned, wise, and kind pastor would sit in his book-lined study with one (or perhaps at most two) parishioners, dispensing the following "basic functions of pastoral care":[15]

◆ Healing
◆ Sustaining
◆ Guiding
◆ Reconciling

While dimensions of each of these are still relevant, and students of pastoral care today are likely to encounter them as normative aspects of

 **The basic functions of pastoral care** as developed by pastoral theologians are: Healing, sustaining, guiding, reconciling, nurturing, empowering, and liberating. It should be noted that none of these activities are within the pastor's capabilities alone, but depend on God and community.

what makes care "pastoral," Carroll Watkins Ali has further expanded these basic functions. Based on her contextual therapeutic stance, grounded in Womanist theology (with a focus on empowering Black women spiritually, emotionally, and physically), as seen in her previously quoted description of her client "Lemonine," she adds these functions:[16]

- ◆ Nurturing
- ◆ Empowering
- ◆ Liberating

## Content: What Is the Scope of Pastoral Care?

On the Emmaus road, as we have seen, Jesus asked his fellow travelers, "What are you discussing?" (Luke 24:17a) He was seeking to understand the pressing concerns and issues that weighed upon their hearts. No less important than understanding something about the surrounding stressors that affect individuals and families in our care is the actual content of issues and problems with which people in congregations are frequently struggling. Thinking back to Aristotle's types of knowledge identified in chapter 1, making referrals encompasses *technē* (technical how-to; knowledge or craft), *epistēmē* (scientific knowledge or knowledge of facts), and *phronesis* (practical wisdom). Every professor of pastoral care will organize an introductory course on pastoral care somewhat uniquely: some will emphasize cultivating the *technē* of how to listen both to the other and to one's inner impulses (countertransference); some will emphasize the *phronesis* of theological and clinical reflection and assessment; others will emphasize the sociological and psychological *epistēmē* of responding to particular issues. (Of course, this is reductive, as all three emphases involve all three kinds of knowledge!) The following is a comprehensive template for what an introductory class will usually cover, with varying emphases:

1. Students will develop an awareness, analysis, and critique of the larger social, economic, gender, racial, sexual, and political contexts in which individuals' and families' pain is addressed in the pastoral-care situation.
2. Students should receive practical grounding in the fundamentals of responding to common pastoral situations (attending illness, death, and dying; home and hospital visitation; premarital preparation/brief marital counseling; spiritual support) as well as common crisis situations (such as addictions, mental illness, and family violence). Carefully chosen books, articles, and films created by experts on specific life challenges and crises will usually serve to amplify classroom discussions.

In addition, most introductory courses offer some practice in specific listening skills, through directed field work, role plays, or in-class listening exercises. Increasingly, "listening" via social media and the Internet will be addressed, as an entire generation of young adults will bring their favored forms of communication with them into pastoral situations—and to seminary!

3. Students will become acquainted with elements of the fields of counseling and psychology as they have been commonly appropriated within the pastoral-care discipline (e.g., understanding basics of couple and family dynamics, psychological health and illness, crisis and addictions, and the normal processes of grief). Some courses will also address new research findings from the growing fields of cognitive science, neurology, and human development.[17] Psychology in a pastoral care course is offered mainly in order to help students learn to make appropriate pastoral assessments of what persons most urgently need, and from whom. The emphasis is on knowing when and how to refer to other professionals, and on building professional networks for more effective and holistic care.

4. Students will develop theological frameworks for understanding their own pastoral identity, the meaning of care of persons, and the pastoral role of Christian community, and for conceptualizing health and wholeness with particular reference to their own theological traditions. Students will learn one or more methods for doing theological reflection on pastoral-care cases.

5. Students will become familiar with concepts of wellness, spiritual health, and keeping good boundaries, with attention to self-care as well as care of others and of the community as an essential aspect of spiritual formation. Related issues of professional ethics will also be addressed. Use of the self in pastoral care and the concept of "countertransference" in the pastoral relationship will be introduced, with opportunities to practice countertransference awareness in both the practicum work and written assignments.

It is beyond the scope of this chapter to cover all the details of these areas of pastoral study, just as it is beyond the scope of an introductory course to cover every one of these dimensions in full depth. It should become apparent, however, that the curriculum for learning practices of pastoral care is far more than a set of skills to be mastered or even a set of psychological theories to be applied in the pastoral setting. All five of these areas actually overlap continually in the ongoing practice of pastoral care, and theological reflection as well as reflection on the needs of the person coming for help and on our own needs and vulnerabilities are in constant interplay. This takes practice, and the guidance and wisdom of our peers and our mentors is essential for learning the art of pastoral caregiving. There are many very helpful books addressing particular issues and problems, including addiction, abuse, mental illness, and more developmental crises such as the pressures of adolescence and the challenges of aging. Part of one's pastoral wisdom is not to have all the answers but to know of books and articles to look them up! Even so, there is absolutely no textbook that can substitute for the value of supervised learning in this field.

## Diversification: Expanding the Circle of Caregivers

Contextualization of pastoral care, with its commitment to relational justice, leads to the fourth aspect of change in pastoral care: diversification. This refers to diversification both of caregivers and of resources in church and community that can be made available to those seeking pastoral help. These matters of resources and making referrals are among the most important practices in pastoral care. Knowing when and to whom to refer is not only common sense—we cannot possibly provide all things to all people even in a small congregation!—but is also a living demonstration of our conviction that we do not have to be the expert in everything, and we trust in the collective wisdom of the community.

However, we do not "refer and dump." Since at times a parishioner can feel a referral to be a brush-off, it's important to convey that we are creating networks of collaboration in the community and widening the circle of care to include people with greater expertise in a particular issue than we ourselves have. Furthermore, it is not our role to be therapist, coach, vocational counselor, school guidance professional, evaluator for learning disabilities, or medical diagnostician. At the same time, it is our distinctive role to provide ongoing spiritual support after a referral to a community resource has been made. Hence, we do not refer and dump, but we refer and support the referral. It is important to follow up and ask how the referral worked out, and to go back to the drawing board as necessary if the first referral did not go well. It is also within the distinctive purview of our own role as spiritual caregivers to continue to reflect together with persons about their larger questions of meaning, purpose, sin, salvation (sometimes called *soteriology*—literally the study of salvation or well-being), and perhaps the most difficult pastoral question of all: why God even allows suffering and

> The reality of **suffering, sin, and evil** poses the most difficult question in pastoral theology. Why do suffering and evil exist if God is both good and all-powerful? Theologians have adopted many varying answers to this central problem, but to grapple with this question of *theodicy* (see text) is a central theme in pastoral care and counseling, and one which confronts both beginning and seasoned pastoral caregivers as life in this world entails grief and sorrow as well as joy.

evil to exist (sometimes called *theodicy*, from *theos* + *dike*, literally to justify God in light of the reality of evil). But even this we need not do alone! Spiritual conversations can take place not only one-on-one in the pastor's study, but also in small groups, house meetings, and other gatherings where church members and friends ponder these mysteries, just as the disciples pondered the mystery of Jesus' death and resurrection in the midst of their grief on the road to Emmaus.

Even the most casual survey of how people care for one another in cultures worldwide and across various ethnic and cultural groups within North America shows that not all pastoral care has ever been dispensed in the one-on-one setting of a professional office with a fixed appointment, nor has all pastoral care ever been dispensed solely by the clergy. The one-on-one model has all too often perpetuated a one-up/one-down expert role that tends subtly to "fix" rather than empower the one coming for help. Even access to such elite helpers has been limited to those with certain social and economic means. However, there is now a growing respect for the wide variety of resources available for pastoral care and for the clergyperson as one resource—albeit an important one with particular gifts—among many. Bonnie Miller-McLemore at Vanderbilt University states that "pastoral care curriculum has focused increasingly on how congregations provide care and on clergy as *facilitators of networks of care*" (emphasis added),[18] rather than sole caregivers. Similarly, pastoral counselor Margaret Kornfeld has written about pastoral care through the gardening metaphor of "cultivating wholeness,"[19] in which a variety of gardeners with a variety of expertise collaborate in the facilitation of spiritual growth and healing of individuals and communities.

Miller-McLemore has revised another paradigm that was widely circulated from the mid-twentieth century, Anton Boisen's idea of the "living human document."[20] In his time, Boisen was concerned that pastoral caregivers turn from an overreliance on theory and texts to a more existential respect for the life of individuals in all their uniqueness. He called for "the study of human documents as well as books,"[21] and his phrase, *living human documents*, struck a resonant chord in pastoral caregivers who sought, legitimately, to get closer to the lived inner experience of their helpees. However, this paradigm, too, was limited by its individualistic bent. Miller-McLemore has proposed replacing the living human document with the *"living human*

---

**We are all inter-connected!** The recent metaphor of the "living human web" is a good image for the pastoral caregiver's view of care as both individual and communal. Resources for care, therefore, include both the pastor and, as appropriate, other persons and agencies—both within the congregation and in the wider community. Care for individuals and families goes hand in hand with advocacy for healing and justice in communities as well.

---

*web"* as the "appropriate subject for investigation, interpretation, and transformation."[22] She advocates for "a shift toward context, collaboration, and diversity,"[23] in which the work of caregiving includes both individual and communal care, respecting the complexity and multiple contextual realities of people's lives. If we consider for a moment the view of our beautiful blue planet as seen from outer space, "this fragile earth, our island home,"[24] it is apparent that we are all connected!

In concrete terms, this means that the notion of care expands from that lone pastoral caregiver in the study with a lone parishioner or couple or even family to a web of resources gathered collaboratively to address the complex, multilayered needs and struggles of the helpee. It means having a list of contacts (whether in an old-fashioned well-thumbed card file or on the latest smartphone). These contacts should be personally known and trusted helpers in the community with varieties of expertise, including spiritual directors, therapists, social workers, school officials and educators, medical professionals, lawyers, financial advisers, public agencies, and community organizers. It means sharing the responsibility and the authority for pastoral care with trained and empowered lay caregivers, such as lay Eucharistic ministers, small-group leaders, Stephen Ministers, parish nurses, and pastoral-care teams. It means hitting the pavement to identify and join with others who are working in the community to change the conditions that perpetuate suffering, and inviting those individuals into our congregations as witnesses to the wider needs of the community.

There is an added benefit to this emphasis on knowing when and how to refer, because although it sounds like a lot, in one way it is actually less taxing than the old paradigm. As we share the responsibility for providing care, we are also much less prone to burn out and therefore are more available to respond to the wide variety of requests that may come to us day by day. In this new more communal paradigm, the pastoral caregiver no longer needs to be seen as having sole responsibility for the welfare of the "flock." This becomes a shared responsibility and a collaboration of the whole body of Christ by virtue of our baptismal covenant, in partnership with the wider community.

## Balance: From Shepherd to Samaritan

This leads to the fifth and last aspect of change: balance. A collaborative approach to pastoral care replaces the old self-sacrificing model of the shepherd with a paradigm of balance, exemplified in care for self as well as others and in a respect for boundaries as a positive good. The image of the oxygen mask on an airplane is a trite but true analogy. The safety announcement on every airliner instructs passengers in case of an emergency to put on one's own oxygen mask first, before assisting another person. If we exhaust ourselves in giving without taking time to replenish, if we burn out, we soon are no use to anyone. We also are not much use to ourselves; our relationships with others and ultimately even with God suffer. We may lose sight of our countertransference, as described earlier in this chapter. When we overextend ourselves on behalf of others, we are prone to falling into the trap of the martyr's self-aggrandizement: "I'm indispensable, I'm so important, everyone needs me!" We don't have time to refuel as we should in prayer and rest and personal self-nurturing activities, and pretty soon we derive our sense of satisfaction and self-worth from those we are helping, rather than from the resources of our own personal lives—and most importantly, rather than from our own nourishing relationship with God.

Pastoral theologian Jeanne Stevenson Moessner has held up the biblical image of the Good Samaritan (Luke 10:25-37) as an alternative to the shepherd paradigm.[25] The Good Samaritan helped the man whom he found on the side of the road, half-dead, stripped, and beaten. But he also went on with his own journey. He did not give up his life for the stranger, but rather shared life with him. And further, he made a referral! He solicited the assistance of another helper—the innkeeper—pledging resources and support, and pledging to return, but also keeping the other commitments of his life. He kept all his commitments in balance! This story, in fact, is a useful example of the power of a good, timely referral to a trusted resource. Nor did the Samaritan refer and dump, but rather, he promised ongoing

**Boundaries and self-care**: The Good Samaritan serves as a helpful metaphor to place alongside the Good Shepherd. Keeping good boundaries, not losing sight of our own purpose, and caring for oneself are crucial to good pastoral care for others. We are called to nourish our own relationship with God, and to love our neighbor as ourselves, but not instead of ourselves. Keeping good balance is a crucial practice of ministry.

support for the referral. All this he accomplished without sacrificing his own plans and without becoming entangled in an enmeshed, dependency relationship inappropriate to the task of care. The message of the Samaritan is simple but poses a healthy alternative to some traditional models of care: share the caring task with other helpers, stay connected but not overinvolved, and stay whole yourself.

Moessner uses the Samaritan story also to illustrate Christ's summary of the law—"love your neighbor as yourself,"—as a paradigm of interconnection among God, self and neighbor.[26] The failure to care for self as well as for others can lead to a further peril beyond burnout; it is a very small step from deriving our self-worth from those we are helping, to beginning to use them to gratify other needs of ours as well—emotional, even sexual. In this way, attention to keeping good boundaries is not withholding appropriate love and care, but rather, safeguarding that love and care within a container of trust, respect, and safety. When we begin to overvalue our own importance in tending the needs of others, and over-identify and confuse ourselves with our role—or, worse, with the Savior—very bad things can happen.

Finally, it is Christ who is the great shepherd of the sheep, not we ourselves. When we cling too hard to the shepherd paradigm, we may run the risk of confusing ourselves with the savior—a temporarily gratifying but ultimately soul-killing proposition for us and for all whom we serve. In the words of the famous doxology, it is ultimately God/Christ/Spirit "from whom all blessings flow": healing, sustaining, guiding, reconciling, nurturing, empowering, and liberating. Trying to provide all these things ourselves not only is a prescription for burnout, but also may simply be another form of countertransference—puffing ourselves up as "special carers"[27] indispensable to others, as a way of bolstering our own faltering self-esteem. This is not a healthy way to practice ministry, nor is it a healthy way to live! And leaning on God to provide for us as helpers is, finally, deeply reassuring and empowering as we try to offer care.

Dorothy McRae-McMahon calls for self-awareness, a certain lightness of being, and a daily vocation based in gratitude toward God and profound respect toward every other person. She writes, "Underpinning all that I do pastorally is the absolute conviction that God is at the bottom of every abyss, is the oasis in the desert, the light in the darkness that is never extinguished, and the waiting meaning in the nothingness." [28]

We are not meant to practice our ministries alone. Jesus sent the disciples out two by two. He did not send individuals, but partners. And when those partners went forth, he foretold that they would be empowered to do great healing works in his name. This is another image that for us serves as a corrective to the paradigm of the shepherd: the image of the disciples going out as partners, without lots of extra provisions, but with the confidence of the gospel and the reliance on the hospitality of strangers that would make their mission possible. In this paradigm, we become companions to one another on the journey, and as we go, we may find ourselves, as did the disciples on the Emmaus road, walking side by side with Christ himself.

## Questions for Personal Exploration

1. What obstacles or distractions might get in the way of your being a helpful listener?
2. Can you cite an example of where another person has projected "their own stuff" onto you? How did you feel, and how do you imagine yourself handling such projections as a pastoral leader?
3. Thinking back on a time when you were hurting or grieving, what did you need from others? What did others do that was helpful, and not so helpful?
4. Recognizing that pastoral care must be appropriate to culture and context, in what ways is this chapter relevant for your own cultural context? What changes or adaptations to your own practices might you make in order to provide culturally appropriate care?
5. Name some of the horizontal and vertical stressors in your personal life and cultural context. What forms of pastoral care would best address them?
6. As a caregiver, do you see yourself as more like the Good Shepherd or the Good Samaritan? Depending on your answer, what might you need to change to keep your life in healthy balance?

 ## Resources for Deeper Exploration

Cooper-White, Pamela. *Shared Wisdom: Use of the Self in Pastoral Care and Counseling.* Minneapolis: Fortress Press, 2004.

Doehring, Carrie. *The Practice of Pastoral Care: A Postmodern Approach*, revised expanded edition. Louisville: Westminster John Knox, 2015.

Hunter, Rodney, and Nancy Ramsay, eds. *The Dictionary of Pastoral Care and Counseling.* Expanded ed. Nashville: Abingdon, 2005.

Moessner, Jeanne Stevenson. *A Primer in Pastoral Care.* Creative Pastoral Care and Counseling Series. Minneapolis: Fortress Press, 2005.

Wimberly, Edward P. *Counseling African American Marriages and Families.* Louisville: Westminster John Knox, 1997.

## 👓 Notes

1. A term that recognizes that the so-called "Third World" actually represents the majority of global citizens.

2. Adapted from Vincent D'Andrea and Peter Salovey, *Peer Counseling: Skills and Perspectives* (Palo Alto, CA: Science and Behavior Books, 1983), 63, citing Joseph Luft, *Group Processes: An Introduction to Group Dynamics*, 3rd ed. (New York: McGraw-Hill, 1984).

3. On gentle confrontation as proclamation in pastoral care, see Charles Taylor, *The Skilled Pastor: Counseling as the Practice of Theology* (Minneapolis: Fortress Press, 1991).

4. For more on congregational dynamics and the projections that occur from a family systems perspective, see Edwin Friedman, *Generation to Generation: Family Process in Church and Synagogue* (New York: Guilford, 1985).

5. For a detailed discussion of both helpful and unhelpful forms of countertransference in pastoral situations, including a related method for theological reflection, see Pamela Cooper-White, *Shared Wisdom: Use of the Self in Pastoral Care and Counseling* (Minneapolis: Fortress Press, 2004).

6. Pamela Cooper-White, *Many Voices: Pastoral Psychotherapy in Relational and Theological Perspective* (Minneapolis: Fortress Press, 2007), 5–7.

7. Margaret Kornfeld, "Change Supported by the Solution-Focused Method," ch. 6 in *Cultivating Wholeness: A Guide to Care and Counseling in Faith Communities* (New York: Continuum, 1998), 114–46.

8. Charles Taylor, *The Skilled Pastor: Counseling as the Practice of Theology* (Minneapolis: Fortress Press, 1991), esp. 65–80.

9. For example, Andrew D. Lester, *Hope in Pastoral Care and Counseling* (Louisville: Westminster John Knox, 1995); Christie Cozad Neuger, *Counseling Women: A Narrative Pastoral Approach* (Minneapolis: Fortress Press, 2001); and Edward P. Wimberly, *African American Pastoral Care*, 2nd ed. (Nashville: Abingdon, 2009).

10. Nicholas Wolterstorff, *Lament for a Son* (Grand Rapids: Eerdmans, 1987), 34.

11. An important twentieth-century psychoanalyst, Heinz Kohut, developed an entire mode of therapy based on the centrality of empathic listening, called Self Psychology. For an application of this specifically to pastoral care, see Chris R. Schlauch, *Faithful Companioning: How Pastoral Counseling Heals* (Minneapolis: Fortress Press, 1995).

12. Carroll Watkins Ali, *Survival and Liberation: Pastoral Theology in African American Context* (St. Louis: Chalice, 1999), 5.

13. Betty Carter, Monica McGoldrick, and Nydia Garcia-Preto, *The Expanded Family Life Cycle*, 4th ed. (Needham Heights, MA: Allyn & Bacon, 2010), 6. (Chart reproduced in this edition from earlier editions by Carter and McGoldrick.)

14. Larry Kent Graham, "From Relational Humanness to Relational Justice: Reconceiving Pastoral Care and Counseling," in *Pastoral Care and Social Conflict*, ed. P. Couture and R. Hunter (Nashville: Abingdon, 1995), pp. 220–34.

15. William A. Clebsch and Charles R. Jaekle, *Pastoral Care in Historical Perspective* (Englewood Cliffs, NJ: Prentice-Hall, 1964), expanding upon Seward Hiltner's *Preface to Pastoral Theology* (Nashville: Abingdon, 1958), 89–174. "Healing" as a basic "function" of pastoral care especially has been critiqued as too individualistic, too focused on a medical model of physical cure, and too disconnected from other dimensions of well-being such as reconciliation with both God and community. See Sharon Thornton, *Broken yet Beloved: A Pastoral Theology of the Cross* (St. Louis: Chalice, 2002), 166–67.

16. Watkins Ali, *Survival and Liberation*, 9.

17. For example, see Felicity Kelcourse, ed., *Human Development and Faith: Life-Cycle Stages of Body, Mind, and Soul,* 2nd ed. (St. Louis: Chalice, 2015); David A. Hogue, *Remembering the Future, Imagining the Past: Story, Ritual, and the Human Brain* (Eugene, OR: Wipf & Stock, 2009).

18. Bonnie Miller-McLemore, "The Living Human Web: Pastoral Theology at the Turn of the Century," in *Through the Eyes of Women: Insights for Pastoral Care*, ed. Jeanne Stevenson Moessner (Minneapolis: Fortress Press, 1996), 14.

19. Kornfeld, *Cultivating Wholeness*.

20. Anton Boisen, *The Exploration of the Inner World* (New York: Harper & Brothers, 1952/1936), 247, also explored in Charles Gerkin, *The Living Human Document: Revisioning Pastoral Counseling in a Hermeneutical Mode* (Nashville: Abingdon, 1973/1984).

21. Boisen, *Exploration of the Inner World*, 10.

22. Miller-McLemore, "The Living Human Web," 16.

23. Ibid., 13.

24. *The Book of Common Prayer* (New York: Church Publishing, 1979), Eucharistic Prayer C, p. 370.

25. Jeanne Stevenson Moessner, "A New Pastoral Paradigm and Practice," in *Women in Travail and Transition: A New Pastoral Care*, ed. Maxine Glaz and Jeanne Stevenson Moessner (Minneapolis: Fortress Press, 1991), 198–225.

26. Ibid., 200. See also Moessner, "From Samaritan to Samaritan: Journey Mercies," in *Through the Eyes of Women: Insights for Pastoral Care*, ed. Jeanne Stevenson Moessner (Minneapolis: Fortress Press, 1996), 322–33.

27. Cooper-White, *Shared Wisdom*, 108, 144, 172–73.

28. Dorothy McRae-McMahon, *Being Clergy, Staying Human: Taking Our Stand in the River* (Washington, DC: Alban Institute), 46.

**Chapter 5**

# Companions in Telling the Story: Practices of Christian Education

Then beginning with Moses and all the prophets, he interpreted
to them the things about himself in all the scriptures.

—Luke 24:27

If you were raised in a Christian tradition, you are likely to have had some experiences that fall into the realm of Christian education. Pamela remembers going to a local church's "Sunday school," where a burned-out volunteer persisted for several years (third grade, fourth grade, fifth grade, . . .) in having the children color maps of Paul's journeys. After having dutifully gone through several boxes of crayons and colored pencils, Pamela came out of this exercise having no idea who Paul really was nor why his journeys were important, but having received training to be a "good girl," able to follow instructions and color inside the lines. Another learning venue there was junior choir, which was more fun but also left no discernible theological traces. Later, in her teen years, Pamela decided to return to the Episcopal Church, her family's denomination, and remembers little from confirmation classes except that, as a girl from the neighboring town with the rival football team, she experienced little fun and a fair amount of shunning in the social activities, and the priest (with somewhat grudging admiration) branded her as "the one who asks questions all the time." The experience of confirmation itself, however, with the laying on of hands by the bishop, has stayed with her to this day as a sacramental experience of grace that strengthened and renewed her relationship with God and the church.

Michael remembers (somewhat more fondly) going through two years of Lutheran confirmation classes in his early teens, during which the stern but kindly pastor, Rev. A. J. Sheldahl, led his small band of confirmands through Luther's catechism, culminating in a medieval-style public examination before the entire congregation. To this day, Michael has the catechist's words "What does this mean?" engraved on his brain and heart. Somewhere along the line, both of us as young adults who had initially set out on other trajectories in graduate school (musicology and the law, respectively) felt drawn toward a vocation of ministry and, along with that, an immersion in theological education.

For Pamela, the genuine sense of drawn-ness began with an interfaith youth group sponsored by a local Congregational church, where the wise youth leaders—a young couple with much love and enthusiasm—allowed a weekly gathering of Catholic, Protestant, and religiously questioning teens to run a folk music coffee house, join in a weekly circle for prayer and singing around a candle, and engage in any questions whatever about faith, feeling, and intellect. Later, immersion in a small blue-collar church as a minister of music caused her to discern a formal call to ordained ministry. But everyone from this original youth group experienced a sense of God's nearness and a particular sense of calling in their lives—two became ordained clergy, one entered religious life as a Little Sister of Jesus, and many more found their ministries in a variety of secular (non-church) occupations.

For Michael, this sense of calling began in his boyhood rural congregation, where a pastor and some lay leaders encouraged him to consider public ministry. Along the way, an opportunity to be a vacation Bible school teacher leading other young persons as they were challenged to grow in knowledge and devotion signaled a possible vocation in the church. This later crystallized through involvement in an avant-garde new mission congregation whose pastor's and key lay leaders' expansive understanding of Christian education included intense discussions of social issues in the era of the civil rights movement and the Vietnam War.

In both our cases, it might be said that much of our Christian journey was "formed" (a word we will return to shortly) in part because of, and in part in spite of, our experiences of formal Christian education. Returning to the Emmaus road, what does the simple sentence in verse 27 about Jesus' interpreting to them from the Scriptures tell us about what "good" Christian education might be, patterned after the Savior's example?

## Christian Education Is Not Just for Women and Children!

While Jesus appeared to relish times with children, on the road to Emmaus he approached two adults and walked beside them to foster their growth and edification. But there is still a strong bias toward the idea that education is primarily for children. Traces of this are reflected in the etymology of the word *pedagogy*, which, although it is now used generally to refer to methods of education for all ages, derives (like *pediatrician*) from *paedeia*, the ancient Greek word for holistic education of children—specifically, in that culture, boys.[1] Back in the post–World War II church boom of the 1950s and '60s, Sunday schools were full of children, and Christian education was largely geared toward them. While this is surely an overgeneralization, a kind of majority view persisted in both Protestant and Catholic congregations that children needed a brief intense indoctrination in the faith so they would grow up in it and adhere to it later in life. Many curricula were developed following the best secular educational models available, to help children learn biblical stories, memorize the most important formulas, including the Lord's Prayer and the Ten Commandments, and otherwise be introduced to key biblical and theological tenets of their specific church tradition.

Despite this general devaluing of adult education, Sunday school was not always just for children. Pamela cherishes several tiny hand-colored "certificates of merit" from the early 1900s, signed in the elegant, spidery handwriting of the time, commending her great-great-grandmother for diligence in "Sunday School" as an adult. Fortunately, in recent decades,

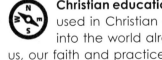 **Christian education is *formation*.** The word *formation* is often used in Christian education to signal that, while we come into the world already in relationship with God who made us, our faith and practices are formed or molded by the Christian community around us, along with the workings of the Spirit in us, in a lifelong process of spiritual growth.

as adult education became a trend in secular educational circles, so "life-long learning" was reclaimed in Christian education as well. This is the idea behind the use of the word *formation* for Christian education—that the journey of faith is a continual process of being molded by the Spirit, with the support of the whole Christian community, into "maturity, to the measure of the full stature of Christ" (Eph. 4:13). We are being "*con*formed [formed together] to the image of Christ" (Rom. 8:29, italics added) and *trans*formed (formed and changed) into the image of "the glory of the Lord" (2 Cor. 18); also, Christ is being *formed* in us (Gal. 4:19). A prominent leader in this reclaiming of lifelong formation, Maria Harris, wrote in 1989:

> Education in the church is lifelong. This is too obvious to bear repetition, too obvious until we begin to see how major are the revisions this belief demands in our educational curriculum. Still, education in the church as lifelong must be our starting point because the pastoral vocation is lifelong. For a people called by the gospel in baptism and confirmation, there is no time in our life when that call ends. Our education into it is ongoing and ought to become increasingly richer and more complex as we develop through adulthood.[2]

In previous generations, Christian education was also considered one of the few proper domains for women in church leadership. While men (both ordained and lay) held roles in church governance, women were assigned to the kitchen, the Sunday school, the nursery, and their own ladies' circles, which were mainly dedicated to socializing, cooking and sewing, and ladylike forms of community service. Since it was the domain of "second-class" members, accordingly, Sunday school and other forms of Christian education were low on the priority list for those who determined budgets. Women interested in full-time ministry as a vocation were steered in the direction of education as an acceptable calling, even as they were steered away from ordination and other forms of church administration, preaching, and leadership.

## Some Fundamentals from Psychology and Educational Theory

Beginning with theologian/psychologist James Fowler in the 1980s,[3] Christian educators and pastoral theologians began to realize the importance of "human development" to understanding persons' growth in faith. Drawing from psychologist Jean Piaget's theories of cognitive development and psychoanalyst Erik Erikson's "eight stages of man,"[4] Fowler identified five "stages of faith" across the life span, in which different modes of thinking at different ages influence both the form and the content of individuals' faith—defined as "our way of finding coherence in and giving meaning to the multiple forces and relations that make up our lives."[5] Christian educators realized that learning could be enhanced by appropriate attention to the different ways in which persons learn at different ages or levels of maturation, and it is their task, at least in part, to help facilitate growth in faith in age-appropriate ways. While it is beyond the scope of this chapter to rehearse all the details of developmental theory, key moments of growth—including growth in the brain itself—determine a child's and adult's capacity literally to put two and two together. Infants' learning is "preverbal," acquired primarily through bodily sensations. Toddlers and very young

---

**Human development and faith**: Christian educators recognize that just as our growth across the lifespan falls into certain recognizable stages or phases, so does our maturation in faith. Education and formation therefore cannot be "one size fits all," and Christian education is not only for children and youth, but should be considered a lifelong endeavor.

---

children tend toward "magical thinking," in which wishes and fantasies are difficult to distinguish from reality. School-age children become very adept at "concrete" thinking, in which facts, "true stories," and rules become prominent. Abstract thinking, however, does not fully come on board until adolescence. Much of what we may take for granted as religious beliefs and ideas, because they are in the realm of spiritual or theological propositions, make absolutely no real sense to a child before the age of twelve or so.

As an example, if we say to five-year-old Dylan that "Jesus died for your sins," he may very well believe Jesus died (probably sometime just last week) because Dylan hit his little brother! While in our mature abstract thinking, we might yet be able to turn that around into a workable theological proposition, the child is not left with reassurance of God's grace, but with the possible fear and guilt that he personally killed Jesus. He's not sure who this Jesus is anyway. He's not so sure about what death means; he never met this "Savior," who is no more real to him than a character in a storybook;

and the resurrection must seem mostly like the experience of "dying" after five attempts to get to the next level on a video game but then, in about twenty minutes, getting a new set of "lives." This is why so many children's sermons can be more enlightening, or at least entertaining, for the adults in the congregation than for the children who march forward (sometimes acting silly because they feel on display) and then trudge back again to their pews, feeling thoroughly confused!

Developmental psychology can obviously take more nuanced and sophisticated forms than the foregoing example. "Stages" of development, especially later in adolescence and adulthood, are not formulaic and do not correspond neatly with particular ages. Many adults remain at so-called earlier stages of reasoning. All of us may "regress" to earlier stages when we are feeling anxious or under threat, while we are able to utilize our full capacities when we are at ease. Like a Russian doll, we all contain all the stages and phases of growth we ever passed through, and all of them still function from time to time in different settings.

Some educators in the 1980s and '90s began doing research into a subfield called moral development, which has had direct crossover into Christian education. Harvard psychologist Carol Gilligan demonstrated that stage theories and researchers' evolving hierarchies of moral reasoning[6] were normed on male research subjects, and that girls' ways of making moral decisions tended to be more relationally based and less grounded on abstract principles alone. Such insights led to challenges to the linear or hierarchical tendency of many developmental stage theories, including the whole framework of "growth" versus "regression," and these critiques have also been brought to Fowler's stages of faith.[7]

The latest frontier in cognitive psychology is the incorporation of the rapidly growing field of neuroscience in learning theory. This, too, is being thoughtfully considered by Christian educators and provides an additional dimension to consider when preparing lesson plans for persons of various ages and cognitive capabilities.[8] Howard Gardner's work on "multiple intelligences"[9] also has been a useful touchstone for thinking about differences not only in learning styles, but also in forms of intelligence that go beyond merely the rational-critical dimension of thought.

Developmental psychology has also shone a light on the differing needs of adolescents and young adults in religious education. In keeping with the old saying that "confirmation is the exit rite," after the blooming years of church attendance in the 1950s and '60s, many church folk were simply happy to keep teenagers involved by any means whatsoever. Often this devolved into socializing as the main focus, with occasional chats about God and Jesus thrown in. Youth leaders today, however, are much more sophisticated in their understanding that faith formation does not end with confirmation. Adults' own hunger for continued theological learning can help us become wonderful partners with teens and younger adults as we explore issues of faith together. Many models for youth ministry are emerging from this recognition. Kenda Creasy Dean and Ron Foster's book *The Godbearing Life*, Tom Beaudoin's *Virtual Faith*, and Benjamin Stephens and Ralph C. Watkins's *From Jay-Z to Jesus* are all examples of thoughtful approaches to ministry with youth and young adults, incorporating sound theological, psychological, and sociological insights with an appreciation for contemporary culture.[10]

This increasingly developmental and sociological approach to Christian formation with youth and young adults has parallels in the emerging-church movement and in the growing use of the Internet and social media.[11] The danger, of course, in merely jumping on a bandwagon of "relevancy" to attract youth where they are is that these trends can become gimmicks, collapsing religious formation into the latest fads in education and evangelism. Naive uses of social media can also put children and adults at risk.[12] But there is potential in these approaches to formation when carried out with critical theological and social reflection.

## Christian Education Is Walking Together

On the Emmaus road, Jesus was walking with the disciples, not charging ahead of them. In 1993, education professor Allison King coined the phrase "from sage on the stage to guide on the side."[13] This pithy saying challenged the lecture approach to pedagogy, which is especially common at the college level. She proposed a more collaborative approach to teaching and learning, including beginning where the students' knowledge was already well grounded, utilizing conversation among students in dyads ("think-pair-share"[14]), and various forms of small-group pedagogy. The role of the teacher shifted from imparting knowledge to facilitating learning. Students in seminary will no doubt still experience both forms of teaching, and lectures are still popular at the college level, especially in very large introductory courses. But as the tide has shifted toward an appreciation for

Christian education is not a matter of putting information and beliefs into students, but rather it is a matter of coming alongside and sharing in **a mutual process of teaching and learning**.

multiple learning styles among students, and even multiple intelligences, there is a general recognition among educators that there cannot be a one-size-fits-all approach to teaching.

This rapidly expanding growth in pedagogical approaches has generated a dizzying number of curricula for children and adults. In our view, the specific curriculum content is therefore not the only thing to evaluate, but also its basic underlying assumptions about what teaching and learning mean for people of all ages. Just as good pastoral care depends on the empathy that comes from genuine listening, so does good educational practice.

Contemporary approaches to Christian education emphasize that it is not only a matter of raising up individuals in the faith, but a mission of the whole community, for the whole community. Norma Cook Everist, for example, offers "a vision of the entire parish as a learning community."[15] She describes a three-part model for holistic education that includes a "cycle of life" (from infancy to older adulthood), "blessings for life" (from baptism through family covenants and the "historic catechumenate"—the ancient patterns of initiation into the Christian community—to retreats and "blessings for discipleship"), and a "peace-teaching model" that focuses on life-long Scripture study, reconciliation, empowering respect, understanding of other cultures, mission activity, and the equipping of leaders.[16] Drawing on Paul's images of differing gifts within the body of Christ, she sees the following goal of Christian education congregation-wide: "Through formation, transformation, and renewal, the Christian faith community is not to be conformed to this world, but is a fully gifted living body of Christ serving the world" through "love, mutual affection, honor, zeal, service, hope, patience, perseverance in prayer, care for those in need, and hospitality to those outside the community."[17]

## Formation Is Inclusive, Intercultural, and Mobile

Jesus' teaching was not limited and restrictive, but the gospel says he interpreted *all* the Scriptures (Luke 24:27). As he would soon underscore for his apostles on the verge of his ascension, they were to go into *all* the world and proclaim the good news to the whole creation (Mark 16: 15). And they were to *go,* in recognition that their continuing formation and their mission would happen on the road. Authentic Christian education and formation today, accordingly, must be inclusive, intercultural, and designed to be available not just "in church" but in multiple locales and venues, including in our homes, at our workplaces, and increasingly via the Internet and other emerging technological spaces.

Contemporary approaches to Christian education, like other practical disciplines, have recognized that in past decades, most pedagogical approaches in U.S. churches unconsciously assumed a white, middle-class American consumerist model that was not equally applicable to all contexts. Sunday school curricula were written and published primarily for churches that could afford them and portrayed a preponderance of images of white children and adults—as well as, all too often, a white European Jesus! In the 1960s and '70s, with the rise of the civil rights movement, immigration, and increasing involvement of churches in forming global partnerships, Christian educators recognized that many curricula and educational theories were too culture bound. As in many other theological

> **Christian education is becoming increasingly multi- and intercultural,** as the North American church itself is recognizing the richness and importance of cultural, gender, and other forms of diversity. One of the aims of formation, then, is to equip Christians for respectful, constructive dialogue amidst difference as one expression of the wholeness of the Gospel message of love and justice throughout the world.

(and secular) fields, multiculturalism became an intentional value.[18] By the 1990s, various forms of diversity and anti-racism training were established as requirements for leaders in many religious denominations. In the field of Christian education itself, senior scholars began to welcome and promote the ethnic and racial diversity of graduate students entering the field, and with the advent of a more diverse group of scholars (both national and international), the field began increasingly to embrace a model of multicultural Christian education. In the words of one educator, "Religious education which is authentically Christian should be as wide as the arms of Christ and embrace with equal warmth persons of every ethnic and cultural group."[19]

Early efforts aimed more at assimilation and a melting-pot ideal have been increasingly critiqued as erasing distinctive differences among cultural and ethnic groups. Today, culturally sensitive Christian education is more appropriately informed by a vision of community in which respect and appreciation for difference is valued. To quote David Ng, in his reframing of the biblical story of the Tower of Babel as a "multicultural vision": "What God has put asunder let no one try to melt into one pot or tower or domicile."[20] This may sound shocking to those who have only been told the story of the Tower of Babel as a negative story of God's punishment for human hubris. Such shocks to the system are in themselves teachable moments, as predominantly white North American churches grapple with their own racism (whether intentional or deeply ingrained, unconscious, and denied).

Ng outlines how "cultural minority churches" and "cultural majority churches" have different tasks in promoting multicultural education. Churches established to reach ethnic populations or racial groups still not welcome elsewhere need to replace a hierarchical strategy of "teacher over learner" with the development of leaders who can "recognize the identity focus of minority people in a majority culture and assist their members to identify themselves as full human beings—people with experiences, histories, and aspirations, with their own validity and integrity. Religious education in such settings must identify study themes that are especially relevant to that ethnic group." White majority congregations, by contrast, "need to learn cultural awareness, including . . . their own 'invisible, weightless knapsacks of cultural imperialism' that must be unpacked."[21]

Most recently, the use of the term *multicultural* itself is being replaced in practical theology by the terms *cross-cultural* and *intercultural*. As Christian educator Rodger Nishioka notes, "Most educators recognize that multicultural education does not teach us to interact with others. Rather, we simply tolerate difference. [That's] not enough in this 21st century."[22] Meeting those who are different from ourselves and who push us beyond the comfort zone of our cherished assumptions—including our religious beliefs—is perhaps the most challenging but most important form of Christian education, in which our faith is stretched to reach as wide as Christ's embrace.

Just as secular educators in the 1960s began to recognize that "education" goes far beyond what happens in classroom and school buildings, Christian educators have also noted that religious formation is not confined to Sunday school. Of course, this is not a new insight. Luther advocated for catechesis in the home, as one of the chief responsibilities of parents toward their children. The Greek word *catechesis* literally means "to echo" or "to hand down," implying oral instruction.[23] Today this ancient word is most often used in connection with baptismal instruction or confirmation but has increasingly been reclaimed from ancient church practices as another form of lifelong education in faith.

Christian education, or formation, thus goes far beyond a Sunday-morning hour-long curriculum. It is as wide as the mission of the whole church. As Maria Harris puts it most concisely, "The congregation does not *have* a curriculum; the congregation *is* a curriculum."[24] We learn not only through formal practices of reading, writing, studying, and reflecting on texts (both scriptural and theological), but also through the very embodied practices of the whole of church life. Christian formation also spills out beyond the walls of any individual church community, because if the gospel is centered in Christ's love for all people, "the understanding that all (not just each) human beings have equal dignity and that all (not just each) human beings have the right to the abundant gifts of the Creator," then Christian education takes us out into the world, drawing "particular attention to the poorest of the poor in every society, namely, women; to the unequal distribution of the world's goods; and to the disproportionate burdens place on the backs of people of color."[25] In some sense, all the practices being discussed in this book—both those that occur within the church's walls and those that move through faith beyond them—fall under the umbrella of Christian formation.

## Learning Begins with Questions

Jesus initiated the conversation with the disciples by asking an open-ended question, an invitation to dialogue: "What are you discussing with each other while you walk along?" (Luke 24:17) They in turn queried him: "Are you the only stranger in Jerusalem who does not know the things that have taken place there in these days?" (24:18) If Christian education is to be more than a transfer of facts and propositions, but a true process of formation that addresses all our multiple intelligences, our emotional life, and our capacity for wonder, then it makes sense that we should begin not with fixed answers, but with questions. In chapter 1, we made the distinction between inductive and deductive approaches to practices of ministry and practical theology. In Christian education specifically, the old deductive approach based on traditional schooling is (sometimes slowly?) giving way to a more dialogical and inductive approach to teaching and learning where questions precede answers—and responses invite further questioning and critical reflection.

As liberationist educator Paulo Freire wrote, "Existence itself [is] an act of questioning."[26] Freire likened traditional education to a "banking" model, in which teachers essentially deposit learning in students, who are subjected to the teacher's absolute authority.[27] Such an approach to Christian education assumes that people must be introduced to God and given enough capital to "purchase" God's favor. But as the founder of the use of the Montessori approach[28] specifically in religious education, Sofia Cavalletti observed of even the youngest believers, "In so many ways the children have shown me that they are [already] capable of deep religious experience, which I believe means a deep relationship with God. They sense God's presence. They understand and enjoy God's closeness."[29]

Whether we are engaged in formation with children, youth, or adults, it is not even *our* questions as teachers that count the most, but the questions we can encourage and engender in those we dare to join on holy ground and "teach." As Cavalletti insists, religious education or catechesis is finally the work of the Holy Spirit, not our doing as teachers. In fleeting moments of recognition that something transcendent is occurring, we move beyond academic-style questions and answers into a realm of inward response, an unfolding that takes time because "it is not us but the Spirit who works within hearts."[30]

## Not Just Minds, but Hearts and Bodies

The Spirit indeed works with hearts. The apostle Paul also reminds us that Christians are to be "transformed by the renewing of your minds" (Romans 12:2a). Education and formation, therefore, must aim to address both our heads and our hearts. Rather than focusing exclusively or primarily on "heady matters," Christian formation efforts should be cognizant of Gardner's "multiple intelligences" previously noted, which include not only the kind of rational, logical intellect that we often associate with the word *intelligence*, but also several others: linguistic, musical, spatial, and bodily-kinesthetic.

In 1995, Daniel Goleman introduced an additional term, "emotional intelligence."[31] Inspired by critiques emerging in the 1990s of traditional IQ testing and its previously unchallenged racial and class biases, Goleman harnessed contemporary brain science to develop a more holistic way of understanding concepts of thinking and success. This had immediate resonance with educators. Goleman considers emotional intelligence to be at the "center of aptitudes for living," including the ability to "rein in an emotional impulse; to read another's innermost feelings; to handle relationships smoothly—as Aristotle put it, the rare skill 'to be angry with the right person, to the right degree, at the right time, for the right purpose, and in the right way.'"[32]

One emotion that can be nurtured beautifully in contemporary Christian education is wonder. Since faith in and love of God begin and end in awe and wonder, the ultimate aim of all Christian education and formation is to enable ourselves and others to move to places where we, like the two who dined with Jesus at the conclusion of their journey, find "our hearts burning within us" (Luke 24:32b). Cavalletti points to this privilege of helping fashion the spaces within which wonder may reign:

> Wonder is not an emotion of superficial people; it strikes root only in the person whose mind is able to settle and rest in things, in the person who is capable of stopping and looking. It is only through a continued and profound observation of reality that we become conscious of its many aspects, of the secrets and mysteries it contains. Openness to reality and openness to wonder proceed at the same pace: As we gradually enter into what is real, our eyes will come to see it as more and more charged with marvels, and wonder will become a habit of our spirit.
>
> All this is extremely important for education in the general sense, but it is perhaps especially so for religious education. When wonder becomes a fundamental attitude of our spirit it will confer a religious character to our whole life, because it makes us live with the consciousness of being plunged into

an unfathomable and incommensurable reality. If we are disposed to reflect on reality in its complexity, then it will reveal itself to be full of the unexpected, of aspects we will never succeed in grasping or circumscribing; then we will be unable to close our eyes to the presence of something or someone within it that surpasses us. Even calling it "the absurd" is also a way of recognizing its immeasurability. But the religious person will break out in a hymn of praise and admiration.[33]

Finally, also, formation occurs not only in the mind and the heart, but in the body. As children work out the stories from the Bible by reenacting them and even making up new scenes, either with small wooden figures or with their own bodies; as young adults converse about matters of life and faith while hiking or preparing food for a soup kitchen; as older adults sit together and share how their life stories and the stories of the faith come together, there is a natural flowing together of learning, meaning making, and spiritual growth. As Jesus quoted the commandment from the Torah (Deut. 6:5), to "love the Lord your God with all your heart, and with all your soul, and with all your mind, and with all your strength," we, too, are called to be engaged with every dimension of our being, as we learn to "love [our] neighbor as [ourselves]" (Mark 12:30-31). Our embodied practices are not just "good deeds"—they are the school for our souls, and forms of living prayer.

## The Core Curriculum Is Always the Christian Story

As we draw near the conclusion of this chapter on ministry practices related to Christian education, you the would-be practitioner (or one already engaged in ministry) may find your head (and heart!) swimming. What am I to do with all these wonderful theories of education, all these insights from psychology and human development experts? What is my role in facilitating formation, whether I am a pastor, a Christian education director, or a choir director or parish musician?

Working with others to create a climate conducive to lifelong learning for all members and spiritual seekers will be a task for all involved in guiding a congregation's or organization's educational life and formation processes. Ensuring that adequate resources—including budget, materials, and most importantly, human resources (teachers, supervisors, musicians, and others)—are made available is a critical leadership task. An additional absolutely essential role of those responsible for stewarding a parish's or other ministry's formation and education is to assure a safe climate for all involved. This involves matters like insisting upon criminal background checks for teachers who will be working with children and youth, as well as providing oversight and means of disciplining or even dismissing individuals who cannot respect boundaries, become abusive, or in other ways compromise the safety and well-being of all involved in the journey of education and formation.

Yet another essential role of those entrusted with responsibilities for Christian education is the selection and/or creation of curricula and a comprehensive program, in response to the fundamental question: What is it that God wants us to learn, and what might be the outcome of a process

---

**The curriculum in Christian education** is more than a set of answers to be taught and learned by rote, but rather, it arises out of the questions posed by persons today in connection with the Bible, the traditions of the church, and their current life situation. **The core curriculum is "the Christian story"** (see text), including how our life story connects with the story of faith. The life of faith itself is a sacred curriculum; a congregation and its leaders teach by what they practice—and the results of those practices—as much as by what they say!

---

of Christian formation? On the Emmaus journey, Jesus had a core curriculum: "Moses and the prophets" and "all the scriptures" (Luke 24:27). A curriculum, perhaps, represents the *technē* level of Christian education (again referring to chapter 1). At the end of the day, Christian educators—whether they are called Sunday school teachers, catechists, or something else—need concrete tools with which to work. Even the most naturalistic Christian Montessori programs utilize beautifully crafted objects to depict Bible stories and liturgical themes and to supply prompts for catechists to use in wondering together with the children.

The word *curriculum*, like the English word *course*, literally means a running-through. When we teach, outlines, syllabi, and lesson plans—whether provided by a commercial publisher or created by a local committee or work group—help us "stay on course." Most Christian education courses in seminary will offer ways of constructing these. A good curriculum or syllabus often has a kind of arc that begins with introductory materials, moves to delving more deeply or building on what has already been explored (as well as utilizing any conflict that might arise as a further opportunity for learning or teachable moment), and finally comes to a way of summarizing, consolidating what has been learned, and even simply saying good-bye to the group that has gathered and honoring the time that has been spent together.

Beyond any specific technical set of lessons is the deeper core curriculum of faith, which, like that of Jesus, is the Christian story. All good curricula in one way or another are created to share and explore this deepest, most central story. The centrality of "story" in Christian education is not accidental. As human beings, we are most prone to share an experience by telling a story about it, and Jesus himself was prone to use parables as a way of getting his most serious points across. The Talmud, too—that ancient repository of Jewish tradition—is full of stories of rabbis and disciples with their pointed jokes and object lessons (learning by observing and experiencing). However, the idea of story as "the Christian story" goes beyond everything being presented in a strictly narrative form. Christian educator Thomas Groome explains:

> Story symbolizes the living tradition of the Christian community before us and around us (the church) as it takes historical expression in a myriad of different forms, all of which constitute "the Christian Story."' These forms include scriptures, traditions, and liturgies; creeds, dogmas, doctrines, and theologies; sacraments and rituals, symbols, myths, gestures, and religious language patterns; spiritualities, values, laws, and expected lifestyles; songs and music, dance and drama; art, artifacts, and architecture; memories of holy people, the sanctification of time and celebration of holy times, the appreciation of holy places; community structures and forms of governance; and so on. The Vision prompted by the Christian Story is ultimately the reign of God—the ongoing coming to fulfillment of God's intentions for humankind, history, and all creation.[34]

This is not to suggest that the content of curriculum is confined literally to the Bible or by extension to matters of liturgy and doctrine. Good curricula make links between these elements of the Christian story and the lives of children, youth, and adults today. One excellent program for teenagers, called the *Journey to Adulthood* (*J2A*), brings together aspects of faith with issues that adolescents face in everyday life. This curriculum names these crucial issues the "4 S's": self, society, sexuality, and spirituality.[35] Young people need to know that it is safe to talk about some of the most difficult issues in their lives, including bullying, sexual harassment, child abuse, cheating and plagiarism, managing social media relationships, making all kinds of hard moral and ethical choices, and wrestling with vocation, which is a form of discerning their own call by God to use their unique gifts in the world. Anti-racism training and sexual-boundary training (now mandatory for leaders in most denominations), as well as ecumenical and interreligious events to raise awareness of community problems or to foster interfaith dialogue and collaboration, also fall appropriately under the umbrella of religious education. Likewise important is offering multiple opportunities for members to reflect upon their Christian stewardship—and while this means more than how we use money, it does mean money, too! Understood in its totality, then, Christian education is a domain not just for explicitly "religious" content, but for all aspects of daily life as a Christian to which the gospel has relevance—and that means everything!

Anne Streaty Wimberly utilizes a model she calls "story-linking" in her book *Soul Stories*:

> [Story-linking is] a process whereby persons connect components of their everyday life stories with the Christian faith story found in Scripture. Participants also connect their personal stories with Christian faith heritage stories of African Americans found outside Scripture. More specifically, persons link with Bible stories/texts by using them as a mirror through which they reflect critically on the liberation and vocation they have already found or are still seeking. This linkage helps persons to discern the liberating activity of God and God's call to vocation—living in the image of Christ—in both biblical and present times.[36]

While Wimberly's approach is specifically developed for African American Christian education, her use of the interplay of personal, cultural, and biblical story as a method of formation is applicable to many diverse contexts and resembles the process of praxis-reflection described as a central method in practical theology in chapter 1.

## Prophetic and Political Curricula (of, by, and for the People!)

When they think of "Christian education," many parishioners, especially those of the baby boom generation or older, probably conjure up images of prim and proper little girls and boys sitting in sunny Sunday school rooms and singing sweet little ditties like "This Little Light of Mine." Quite a different image comes to mind for the authors as we think of the courageous Christians we have journeyed with on dusty roads in Central and South America, where Christian formation and faithful living mean daily risking one's very life. In dirt-floor huts and tin-roofed shelters throughout the Two-Thirds World,[37] gutsy men and women (with the latter in the majority) engage in what is described in Spanish as *educación popular*. The Spanish word *popular* does not mean "popular" in the way we use that word in English; rather, it means "of, by, and for the people,"[38]—especially for people who are poor, malnourished, and often under siege by criminals or their own governments. Holistic Christian education—which embraces all of life, as we have seen—must move beyond personal growth to communal engagement in the joys and struggles of life in every time. In that sense, it is both prophetic (giving voice to God's word) and political (from the Latin *polis*, which means, simply, the people).

Theologian Edward Farley in recent years mounted a strong argument against the tendency in Christian education—and more generally in all practices of religion—to collude with what he calls "popular piety," rather than meeting the deepest questions of human life with equally deep and serious expressions of faith. Farley contends that much religion, and perhaps especially Christian education, fears a loss of social vitality if it runs too counter to the "quasi-religious civil pieties of the larger culture."[39]

Far from being popular and gaining favor with the powers-that-were in his day, Jesus' curriculum was subversive for the sake of proclaiming God's liberation. Jesus boldly introduced lesson after lesson about God's realm of peace and justice, quoting from the prophet Isaiah:

> "The Spirit of the Lord is upon me,
>> because he has anointed me
>>> to bring good news to the poor.
> He has sent me to proclaim release to the captives
>> and recovery of sight to the blind,
>>> to let the oppressed go free,
> to proclaim the year of the Lord's favor." (Luke 4:18-19)

This was an eschatological curriculum (see chapter 1 for a definition of eschatology) and truly one of good news (the literal meaning of the Old English word *godspel*, an exact parallel to the Greek *euangélion*), declaring that God's reign of liberation for the poor and the marginalized was "at hand"— indeed, had already arrived and was ready to be perceived and lived. It was a lesson plan suffused with the hope of the paradoxically "already-not-yet[40] future of God's fulfillment of the entire world. The praxis of faith, then, following that word of hope, is to live into that very paradox of the already-not-yet—that even though at times the world seems little changed from the violence of ancient times, salvation truly has already come through God's infinite, surrounding presence, through the gift of Christ's incarnation/life in human flesh, and through the gift of the Holy Spirit's ongoing guidance and consolation. Now it is up to us to live it and be it.

Pastoral theologian Edward P. Wimberly describes this in terms of God's unique vocation (literally "calling," from the Latin *vocare*, to call) to each and every person in creation: "The ultimate end of growth facilitation is participation in the unfolding drama of God's salvation. The purpose of the eschatological community is to make people ready to assume their roles and vocations in God's salvation endeavor."[41] A helpful guide for adult vocational discernment in small groups is Suzanna Farnham's *Listening Hearts: Discerning Call in Community*.[42] As this small book makes clear, discernment of call is not only for the ordained or those contemplating ordained ministry! It is for everyone. We are all called by God.

Wimberly's use of the term *growth facilitation* is perhaps the best understanding of the term *formation*—that through our engagement with the stories of our faith as told both in the Bible and in the ongoing witness of our Christian foremothers and forefathers over two thousand years, our lives, too, can be shaped in a Godward direction. We are formed by both being and doing as we, too, like the disciples on the Emmaus road, seek answers to our deepest, most heartfelt questions, listen to the faith-wisdom passed down through the centuries, and walk alongside our teachers, students, and friends as we ponder the Word made flesh and share in the sacred hospitality of the Eucharistic meal.

##  Questions for Personal Exploration

1. If you experienced Christian education as a young person, what moments led to your growth in faith, and were there any that hindered it?
2. In what ways does your congregation treat children and youth as full members of the body of Christ, and how might there be improvement?
3. Thinking about Gardner's concept of multiple intelligences, how would you describe how you learn best? In what ways might you reach out as a teacher to those with other learning styles?
4. If you can recall a story or incident when a teacher (maybe yourself!?) "bombed" and really missed the mark, what led to such disconnect between teacher and learners? What might have helped things to have gone better?
5. This chapter highlights the difference in approach between telling (or "banking") and wondering together. Which approach have you most experienced as a learner, and which resonates best for you as a teacher?
6. What are your own practices in lifelong learning in faith? And what theological education are you most deeply seeking now?

##  Resources for Deeper Exploration

Cavalletti, Sofia. *The Religious Potential of the Child: Experiencing Scripture and Liturgy with Young Children.* 2nd ed. Chicago: Liturgy Training, 1992.

Dean, Kendra Creasy, and Ron Foster. *The Godbearing Life: The Art of Soul Tending for Youth Ministry.* Nashville: Upper Room, 1998.

Dykstra, Craig. *Growing in the Life of Faith: Education and Christian Practices.* 2nd ed. Louisville, Westminster John Knox, 2005.

Harris, Maria. *Fashion Me a People: Curriculum in the Church.* Louisville: Westminster John Knox, 1989.

Pazmiño, Robert W. *Foundational Issues in Christian Education: An Introduction in Evangelical Perspective.* 3rd ed. Grand Rapids: Baker Academic, 2008.

Wimberly, Anne Streaty, and Evelyn Parker. *In Search of Wisdom: Faith Formation in the Black Church.* Nashville: Abingdon, 2003.

## ◔◑ Notes

1. *Paidós* ("child") + *agōgós* ("guide"), from *ágō* ("lead"). Douglas Harper, *Online Etymology Dictionary*, http://www.etymonline.com/index.php?term=pedagogue.

2. Maria Harris, *Fashion Me a People: Curriculum in the Church* (Louisville: Westminster John Knox, 1989), 38.

3. James Fowler, *Stages of Faith: The Psychology of Human Development and the Quest for Meaning* (San Francisco, Harper & Row, 1981). For a somewhat different perspective on human development and faith, see also James Loder, *The Logic of the Spirit: Human Development in Theological Perspective* (San Francisco: Jossey-Bass, 1998).

4. Jean Piaget, *The Moral Judgment of the Child* (New York: Free Press, orig. pub. 1932); Erik Erikson, *Childhood and Society*, 2nd ed. (New York: Norton, 1950).

5. Fowler, *Stages of Faith*, 4.

6. Especially the work of Lawrence Kohlberg, on whom Fowler also drew for *Stages of Faith*; for example, Kohlberg, *The Philosophy of Moral Development* (San Francisco: Harper & Row, 1981).

7. For example, Craig Dykstra and Sharon Parks, eds., *Faith Development and Fowler* (Birmingham, AL: Religious Education, 1986).

8. For example, Jerry Larsen, *Religious Education and the Brain: A Practical Resource for Understanding How We Learn about God* (New York: Paulist, 2000).

9. Howard Gardner, *Frames of Mind: The Theory of Multiple Intelligences*, 10th ed. (New York: Basic, 1993).

10. Kenda Creasy Dean and Ron Foster, *The Godbearing Life: The Art of Soul Tending for Youth Ministry* (Nashville: Upper Room, 1998); Tom Beaudoin, *Virtual Faith: The Irreverent Spiritual Quest of Generation X* (San Francisco: Jossey-Bass, 2000); Benjamin Stephens and Ralph C. Watkins, *From Jay-Z to Jesus: Reaching and Teaching Young Adults in the Black Church* (Valley Forge, PA: Judson, 2009).

11. On the emerging-church movement, see Phyllis Tickle, *Emergence Christianity: What It Is, Where It Is Going, and Why It Matters* (Grand Rapids: Baker, 2012). On the Internet and social media, see Meredith Gould, *The Social Media Gospel* (Collegeville, MN: Liturgical, 2013).

12. For guidance in the safe use of the Internet and social media, see the policy developed by the United Church of Christ Conference and Episcopal Diocese of Connecticut. Episcopal Diocese of Connecticut, "Safe Church Guidelines for Social Media," October 6, 2009, http://www.ctepiscopal.org/content/safe_church_guidelines_for_social_media.asp.

13. Alison King, "From Sage on the Stage to Guide on the Side," *College Teaching* 41, no. 1 (1993): 30–35.

14. Ibid., 31.

15. Norma Cook Everist, *The Church as Learning Community* (Nashville: Abingdon, 2002), 11.

16. Ibid., 208.

17. Ibid., 205–6.

18. Barbara Wilkerson, "Goals of Multicultural Religious Education," in *Multicultural Religious Education*, ed. Barbara Wilkerson (Birmingham, AL: Religious Education Press, 1997), 12.

19. James Michael Lee, personal communication, quoted in Barbara Wilkerson, introduction to *Multicultural Religious Education*, 4.

20. David Ng, "Impelled toward Multicultural Religious Education," *Religious Education* 87 (1992): 193–94, cited in Wilkerson, "Goals of Multicultural Religious Education," 22.

21. Ibid.

22. Rodger Nishioka, personal communication, Aug. 16, 2014, used by permission.

23. Thomas Groome, *Christian Religious Education: Sharing Our Story and Vision* (San Francisco: Jossey-Bass, 1980), 29.

24. Harris, *Fashion Me a People*, 174.

25. Ibid., 28.

26. Quoted in Carol Lakey Hess, "Religious Education," in *Wiley-Blackwell Companion to Practical Theology*, ed. Bonnie Miller-McLemore (Malden, MA: Wiley-Blackwell, 2012), 299.

27. Paulo Freire, *Pedagogy of the Oppressed*, trans. Myra Bergman Ramos (New York: Continuum/Seabury, 1974), 57–74.

28. Maria Montessori was a pioneer in educational reform, beginning in Rome in the early twentieth century. Her work has led to a worldwide movement of Montessori schools and educational practices. See E.M. Standing, *Maria Montessori: Her Life and Work* (New York: Penguin/Plume, 1998).

29. Cavalletti, *The Religious Potential of the Child: Experiencing Scripture and Liturgy with Young Children*, 2nd ed. (Chicago: Liturgy Training, 1992), 17–18.

30. Ibid., 95, paraphrasing Rom. 5:5.

31. Daniel Goleman, *Emotional Intelligence*, 10th anniversary ed. (New York: Bantam, 2005).

32. Ibid., xiii.

33. Cavalletti, *The Religious Potential of the Child*, 139.

34. Thomas Groome, *Sharing Faith: A Comprehensive Approach to Religious Education and Pastoral Ministry—the Way of Shared Praxis* (San Francisco: HarperSanFrancisco, 1991), 139.

35. LeaderResources, "Journey to Adulthood (J2A)," www.leaderresources.org. See also sample pages at http://leaderresources.org/sites/default/files/J2A_Sample_Pages_032411.pdf.

36. Anne Streaty Wimberly, *Soul Stories: African American Christian Education* (Nashville: Abingdon, 1994), 13.

37. A revision of the term *Third World* to indicate that two-thirds or more of the global population actually lives there. Vinay Samuel and Christopher Sugden, *Lambeth: A View from the Two-Thirds World* (London: Morehouse, 1990).

38. Prepositions used by Abraham Lincoln in his famous Gettysburg address.

39. Edward Farley, *Practicing Gospel: Unconventional Thoughts on the Church's Ministry* (Louisville: Westminster John Knox, 2003), 120.

40. Term originally from Oscar Cullman, *Christ and Time: The Primitive Christian Conception of Time and History* (Philadelphia: Westminster, 1964), 7 et passim; see also Michael Cooper-White, *The Comeback God: A Theological Primer for a Life of Faith* (Minneapolis: Augsburg Fortress, 2009), 6–10.

41. Edward P. Wimberly, *Counseling African American Marriages and Families* (Louisville: Westminster John Knox, 1997), 7.

42. Suzanne G. Farnham, *Listening Hearts: Discerning Call in Community*, 2nd ed. (New York: Morehouse, 2011).

## Chapter 6

# Called to be Servants: Practices of Leadership

> As they came near the village to which they were going,
> he walked ahead as if he were going on. But they urged him
> strongly, saying, "Stay with us, because it is almost evening
> and the day is now nearly over."
> —LUKE 24:28-29

As the travelers drew near to Emmaus, Jesus appeared to be going further. But his companions implored, "Stay with us." In those three words, they issued him a call! So too are today's ministers—be they ordained pastors or priests, deacons or deaconesses, or ministers of music, education or youth and family—typically regarded as being "under call." Depending upon one's tradition, there will be different understandings of the nature of that call and how those serving in one capacity (often described as "office") of ministry relate to staff colleagues and laity who fulfill other calls. But regardless of the exact nature of the call and the job description one is invited to fulfill, every public minister is expected to be a leader within the community of faith. When one is issued a call to "stay with us" by a faith community, a dimension of the staying includes ministerial practices often viewed within the broad category of administration. When we set out on the journey of ministry, we cannot predict where we will be called in the future; we will be asked to navigate into uncharted terrain. This final chapter will explore some themes related to faithful leadership and stewarding administrative responsibilities.

Many who contemplate a ministerial calling and some who have served for a prolonged period in public ministry are uncomfortable with the word *leadership*. Critiques from those who have experienced domination under patriarchal leaders must be heard and heeded: while "leader" implies that there are "followers," the ideal named by Jesus is the mature mutuality of "friends" (John 15:15). Thus, the faith community in its global totality may be in search of new terminology, images, and paradigms to describe those who serve in callings we generalize as public ministry. Until such new revelations and linguistic revisions occur, however, there are dimensions of our callings that many will describe under the broad banner of "practices of leadership."

While by no means unique in ecclesiastical circles, the concept of "servant leadership" has emerged as one that addresses some of these critiques and perhaps rests more comfortably on the shoulders of many pastors, priests, and public ministers.[1] Among the many images lifted up by Jesus for his followers to emulate, his exhortation in Matt. 20:26 is primary: "It will not be so among you [lording it over one another]; but whoever wishes to be great among you must be your servant." Traditional symbols worn or carried by many ministers convey visually the kind of leadership we are called to exercise. The stole worn by many ordained clergy is a yoke, conveying that one is "in the harness," helping propel a faith community rather than sitting atop the wagon, cracking the whip for others to do one's bidding. The crozier (staff) carried by bishops in some traditions is a shepherd's crook, a symbol of loving guidance. In the ordination or consecration of deacons and deaconesses, a basin and towel are often presented, recalling how Jesus took towel and basin to wash his disciples' feet before the Last Supper with them.

## Context Again!

In many questions of church administration and leadership, the best answer will frequently be, "It depends." The way one responds to various situations, the manner in which one exercises leadership will vary greatly depending upon both context and the particular "constituency" being served. While a servant leadership style of empowering and enabling others should be a default position for public ministers, there are occasionally circumstances under which only a highly directive take-charge style is appropriate. In times of crisis—if a fire breaks out, if a tornado is bearing down on the church during worship, or if people are somehow endangered—barking orders and demanding immediate obedience to safety instructions are the only responsible course of action. However, in more normal times and in ministry among adults and responsible young people as well, a more democratic form of shared leadership will be the norm for most of us.

Perhaps the issue here is one of genuine authority. There is a distinction between the words *authoritative* and *authoritarian*. Leadership entails legitimate power that is authorized by the congregation or community and that depends on a mutual contract of respect and honesty. Such legitimate power is open, communicative, and transparent (with the exception of personnel matters and pastoral confidentiality). Leaders who are authorita*tive* listen as much as they speak, and exercise shared deliberation as much as possible. Leaders who are authoritative can also healthily confront those who would exercise covert, manipulative power without an authorized contract for leadership. Authorita*rian* leaders tend to use efforts to control as a means of reducing their own anxiety about disorder and conflict. To be sure, a chaotic environment can be destructive. However, as Margaret Wheatley has pointed out, nature has a way of moving through chaos to new creation. She affirms through studies of nature and chaos theory that managing anxiety by nurturing relational webs of connectedness is preferable to—and more effective than—exercising heavy-handed domination.[2]

While such a communal egalitarian ethos is signaled by Jesus' decree that "it [hierarchical domination] shall not be so among you," there are, of course, arenas of ministerial practice in which democratic decision making is not the preferred modus operandi. Issues that are either trivial or highly divisive (especially where justice is involved) as well as emergencies may call for a more directive stance. Some additional scenarios in this regard involve determining the boundaries of responsibility and authority vis-à-vis what are commonly called pastoral acts. While congregations are wise when they develop policies regarding church weddings (scheduling, use of facilities for receptions, whether or not alcoholic beverages and smoking are allowed on church premises, fees for custodian services and musicians, etc.), in most denominations the final determination of who may be married (based upon an assessment gained through confidential premarital counseling) is left to the officiating minister(s). This is an arena in which conflict is growing currently as more and more states permit gay and lesbian couples to marry, and some congregations and denominations are presuming to intrude on pastoral discretion by forbidding clergy to preside at same-sex ceremonies.

Ministerial leadership styles and stances vary considerably with differing expectations based upon a congregation's or denomination's polity and piety. In churches with a highly "congregational" polity, most decisions are made locally with little or no reference to policies, procedures, and governing documents of larger ecclesiastical bodies. By contrast, in churches of denominations whose self-understanding is centralized or "episcopal" (where bishops exercise considerable influence), many decisions remain the prerogative of the local congregation, but others must be in consultation and conformity with policies, procedures, and even canon law established by a regional or national church body. Our own respective service as Episcopal and Lutheran clergy means, for example, that we are not entirely free agents when it comes to the place and terms of our callings. When we have moved from one ministry setting to a new one over the course of our careers, our decisions to do so have always involved close consultation with our bishops in addition to exploratory conversations with search committees.

Other contextual factors that will exert strong influence upon a minister's leadership style involve factors such as congregational (or for non-parish ministers, organizational or institutional) size, setting, history, staffing pattern, and relative health or dysfunction. While the majority of parish clergy, for example, are expected to be generalists who conduct all aspects of ministry with relative competence, those who serve in team ministry on a large staff may be able to specialize and focus more intensely in areas where they have particular interest and competence. In this regard, descriptions such as "youth minister," "visitation pastor," or "minister of music" signal an individual's primary arena of leadership; leadership in other areas will largely fall to other colleagues. The ministry setting will also govern aspects of how visitation and pastoral care are carried out. In most urban and suburban contexts, it is inadvisable to make spontaneous drop-in visits upon parishioners; what used to be regarded as pastoral home visitation is now regarded by many parishioners as home invasion! At the other extreme, in rural communities, ministers who do *not* routinely pay unscheduled visits to the local coffee shop where folks hang out may be perceived as uncaring and "uppity." Furthermore, growing numbers of people of all generations insist upon Internet access and communicate with email and texting, but in some contexts, all-member communication efforts must still include telephone trees, "snail mail," and other more traditional media. Similar cultural and contextual differences shape expectations of and about public ministers in terms of our attire, formality or informality of address, and presentation of a "professional" demeanor. We are not suggesting that ministers be chameleons whose priority is always to please others, but simply noting that such contextual factors have an impact and should be explored carefully, particularly if one is engaged in intercultural settings.

## Neither Command and Control nor Total Chaos

Faith communities are unique among human organizations. While typically they include elements similar to those of a for-profit business (for example, owning real estate, having employees and budgets, and requiring insurance), churches are not commercial enterprises. Ecclesial communities also share many factors common to other not-for-profit service organizations, but they differ in some fundamental ways from these other "charities."

Those who lead congregations need to be aware that they are volunteer organizations by and large. While most churches have one or more paid staff members (and in this regard, ministers are employees), the bulk of the work is accomplished by willing volunteers. Where some ministers go astray is in assuming they have a degree of command and control with volunteers, similar to the authority exercised by a small-business owner over her employees or a corporate supervisor held accountable for the performance and productivity of individuals and work teams. When volunteers fail to fulfill their responsibilities or when they carry out tasks with subpar performance or even damaging results, they can rarely be fired or demoted, as is the case in business, military organizations, or even some other nonprofit organizations. A servant leader in a faith community motivates, influences, and guides the work of others primarily by persuading, coaching, affirming, and expressing appreciation.

In many congregations, the paradigm of volunteers has been replaced entirely by a paradigm of vocations (callings). Church members are encouraged to pray and discern with others to what ministry they are called, both within the church and beyond. They discover places to utilize their gifts and talents. The emphasis is on individuals' growth in faith and discipleship, not on desperately filling holes on committees and teaching rosters. In the experience of the leadership in those congregations, most of the "holes" nevertheless were filled—by people who were eager to participate, rather than weary repeaters who grudgingly filled a position. In the rare situation where certain positions could not be filled following this philosophy, the particular ministry program was reevaluated: If no one feels called to host a women's breakfast or youth bowling trip, are these things we are still committed to doing, or is there another way to accomplish our overall mission that gives rather than drains people's energy?

A faith community cannot be allowed to devolve into a state of chaos where unhealthy dynamics and a few power-hungry persons can cause conflict and create an unsafe climate. As we have served and consulted with congregations and other organizations and ministries over many years, we have witnessed situations where people are seriously wounded as a result of unrealistic egalitarian notions that "We're all equal in all regards, and everyone's opinions are valid and should be heeded." On certain matters—such as insisting upon policies that protect children, youth, and adults from sexual harassment and abuse; requiring financial audits; and ensuring effective separation of duties when it comes to depositing offerings and fiscal record keeping—ministers who take a totally hands-off approach may be enabling bullies, abusers, or embezzlers who can do great damage to individuals and the corporate body.

Within the unique volunteer organization that is a local church or larger ecclesial entity, those who exercise power are often hard to identify. Particularly in smaller congregations with extended families as members, there may be powerful influence on the part of one or two patriarchs or matriarchs. Such individuals may exercise enormous impact even though they fill no office and have no formally identified leadership role whatsoever. After serving in a place for a while, some ministers can be heard to say things like "In my church, nothing happens without Aunt Wilma's assent" or "If John Moneybags doesn't nod his head in the annual meeting, forget about getting many 'yes' votes on a new initiative."

Another dimension of parish dynamics is that there are multiple "dual relationships" and, in many contexts, potential or actual conflicts of interest. A dual relationship exists when one person has a measure of authority or power over another individual under some circumstances, and then the roles are reversed or somewhat leveled in others. For example, a pastor or priest preaches the word of God, presides at the sacraments, and declares forgiveness of sins on Sunday morning (talk about power!). Then in the meeting of the council, vestry, or session on Monday evening, the pastor or priest gives a report and is notified of next year's salary as an employee of the church governing board. A priest counsels a couple concerning their pain and anxiety about not being able to get pregnant and then sits with them both on a committee to plan the children's Christmas pageant, where others are puzzled by the couple's vehement opposition to having a live baby in the manger. A woman pastor is told confidentially by a female parishioner that her husband is beating her, and then the pastor is confronted angrily by the husband, who opposes plans to increase security at the parsonage or manse. These scenarios bring confidential information into dynamic interplay or even conflict with the tasks at hand and/or the pastor's ability to remain a "nonanxious presence"[3] while managing them.

Conflicts of interest can also occur when an individual may stand to realize personal gain from decisions in which she or he participates in an official capacity. If, for example, an attorney is a member of the parish council and is engaged in a professional capacity by the council, that lawyer stands to profit from a decision that will require billable legal counsel. In certain relatively isolated contexts in particular, such dual relationships and conflicts of interest are challenging to avoid. A minister in a remote Alaskan village may not find another doctor or dentist than the one who is member of the parish. Or in some communities, there may be only one reliable contractor (a parishioner) who can renovate the fellowship hall at a fair price. Under such circumstances, broad transparency and open communication are especially important. As long as they are aboveboard and publicly disclosed, conflicts of interest do not always prohibit a professional relationship between a church and its members and ministers.

Even more challenging are some of the questions that come up with regard to minister-parishioner friendships. Can a clergyperson ever be "just a friend" with one who is entrusted to her or his spiritual care? Again, while there are many gray areas and few hard-and-fast rules, it is important for us to be very clear about professional boundaries. One important dimension of understanding pastoral authority is the issue of unequal power and authority when it comes to interpersonal and emotional matters. A minister under call to serve a congregation or other faith community can never step out of her or his pastoral responsibilities and professional relationship with parishioners.

Such matters rise to particularly acute levels when a single minister may develop romantic feelings for an unattached parishioner. Expectations in this regard vary among ecclesial bodies and in their policies, but the general consensus has been moving toward strong discouragement if not outright prohibition of minister-parishioner dating, and it is beyond question in the case of formal pastoral counseling or therapeutic relationships. Our stance is "just say no" to such feelings and maintain very clear boundaries, because there is an irrevocable power differential between pastor and parishioner, even between apparently mature adults, that takes place mostly at the level of unconscious transference and countertransference dynamics (see chapter 4). Even when we, as leaders, may not feel very powerful—or even feel downright powerless—we cannot control the unconscious projections and transference of those in our care. Such uneven power is a poor foundation for an intimate love relationship of equality and mutuality.[4] These ethical mandates may raise many questions and much anxiety, which cannot be fully answered here. Most seminarians will be required to attend trainings on professional ethics and sexual boundaries, which are also required for clergy and lay leaders in most denominations, and these are opportunities to share concerns about these and many other ethical matters.

## Planning: Discerning the Way

While a casual first read of the Emmaus story suggests that the three who traversed the road from Jerusalem were on a relaxed meandering evening trek, they did have a destination—presumably home for the two joined along the way by Jesus—at which they arrived in time for dinner. In our experience, so many congregations or other organizations falter on their journey and often end up in serious conflict for lack of even basic planning. As we have described in more detail in other publications,[5] there continues to be fairly widespread resistance to planning in churches, much of which is fueled by a piety suggesting that human planning might inhibit the free movement of the Holy Spirit. Yet even churches with highly charismatic theologies seem to thrive and prosper best when they develop mission plans, devise effective communication strategies, envision the future state of things, and implement programs that reach people in their mission fields.

Aids to planning are plentiful, including those tailored to ecclesial contexts, which include suggested Bible studies, prayer circle focus groups, and similar resources. Often lacking in such materials, however, is sufficient focus on what is called "environmental scanning." At an early stage in any planning process, those who are involved need to ask some fundamental questions: What is the nature of our context? Who lives in our immediate community? What are their needs, gifts, aspirations, and anxieties? How is our impact area changing, and what do forecasters project for five and ten or more years in the future? This phase of a planning process offers opportunity to expand one's network by tapping the expertise of those who have

 **Parish leaders can glean from common practices in preparing missionaries** for international service. Such preparation typically includes language study (which may be applicable domestically in terms of learning regional idioms, for example), orientation to the local culture(s), and tips for maintaining healthy personal and family relationships in a new and unfamiliar setting. To plan for effective ministry in any context, particularly if it takes us outside our comfort zones, requires this same kind of attentiveness to scanning the environment and getting to know the "mission field."

their fingers on the pulse of a community. Municipal, county, or school district planning personnel, for example, can share with a planning group a wealth of expertise—and they usually will be eager to do so and offer it at no cost. A great deal of demographic data on any city, town, or rural community is now available through Internet sources; again, data from the U.S. Census Bureau and other governmental sources typically can be accessed for no charge.

Beyond gathering and analyzing this type of hard data readily available for almost any context, environmental scanning should include face-to-face encounters with individuals and groups a congregation or other ministry may hope to reach. While door-to-door surveys may be difficult to conduct in many settings these days, and can be counterproductive if received by neighbors as intrusive or invasive, casual drop-in visits at local gathering spots can yield a wealth of wisdom from the people who inhabit any community. Similarly, requests to meet with local officials and leaders of grassroots community groups can develop new friendships and mutually beneficial partnerships. Church leaders can draw valuable insights from practitioners and authors in a field of public service often referred to as community organizing (or CO for short). A number of national CO entities now regularly offer intensive clergy training seminars and workshops that can assist ministers, rabbis, imams, and other religious leaders both in leading their parish or organization and in becoming more effective and engaged citizens.[6]

Complementing a scan of the external environment or community context in which a congregation or ecclesial organization exercises its ministry is an internal focus on key trends, issues, and challenges faced currently and anticipated in the future. Such internal analysis is often conducted by means of a simple process captured in the initials SWOT. Through a SWOT process, a group of astute members can quickly identify perceived strengths and weaknesses within the organization. Then by means of a "bifocal" layer of analysis, a planning group goes on to identify opportunities to expand mission and service, both with existing members and nonparticipants who might be drawn in at some point in the future, and internal and external threats that could impede, diminish, or in extreme cases even destroy a

---

**"Asset-mapping" a variation on SWOT analysis:** A potential pitfall in utilizing the SWOT approach (which analyzes an organization's internal strengths and weaknesses, together with the external opportunities and threats) faced is that a planning group can rush to focus on the weaknesses and threats. An alternative approach, which has gained widespread credibility in recent years, is called "asset-mapping." This approach to planning begins by focusing on the God-given assets or gifts that are present in each individual and every community.

---

ministry. We also highly commend a planning approach called "asset mapping," which begins by identifying and celebrating the gifts and assets present in a congregation or other community.[7]

Following a process of environmental scanning and analysis by means of a SWOT or other process, major and relatively minor possible new directions may begin to emerge. If a faith community does not already have a succinct and up-to-date mission statement, one might be developed as a way of focusing and coalescing around a communal self-identity that most members can embrace. At this phase of planning, some overarching goals might emerge, and working toward them is staged by attaching time lines and assigning implementation responsibilities to individuals and groups.

In a dynamic community, planning is never-ending. The process of discerning what God is calling us to do now and next month and next year will never be concluded, for there is always next month and next year! While the work of planning can thus begin to feel burdensome after a while, if it is employed carefully, ongoing planning can also be a great blessing. If we have established specific plans (journey to Emmaus), we can celebrate when we get there. If we set some concrete goals (renovate the worship space over the next two years) but the objective is not achieved according to plan, we can still make midcourse corrections and redouble efforts. Sometimes, too, the explicit plan to which everyone agrees will fail because there is a contrary unconscious agenda that requires unpacking. When plans repeatedly fail, the use of an outside consultant can be helpful because he or she may be able to identify dynamics—sometimes intergenerational—in which the regular members and leaders are too embedded to name. A pastor may also benefit from a professional consultant or coach who can help with seeing the forest for the trees.

We served as consultants to one congregation's leadership team in which the stated goal was church growth. Lay leaders were frustrated because it seemed that "as soon as a few new members join, others leave and we are still stuck where we are." In the course of a weekend retreat, through many group exercises, it emerged that the church could not grow beyond the pastor's capacity to know each and every member intimately. He carried a beeper 24/7 (a red flag for needing to be needed!) and was exhausting himself responding to every call as if it were an emergency—even to literally rescuing a widow's wayward cat from a tree—repeatedly! We gently posed questions that allowed the pastor to admit to his own exhaustion and validated his considering making a role shift from a "shepherd" to a "rancher."[8] Amid tears, a lay leader of the congregation confessed to feeling a call to ordained ministry, but she had felt inhibited from exploring it because she was afraid she was too needed by her present congregation. Others applauded her revelation and strongly encouraged her to pursue this sense of call. What we all learned was that the favored mode of being in this congregation was to be needed by others, even self-sacrificially needed (with the subliminal gratification that accompanied this). Lifting this to awareness was the first step in addressing the failure of the stated goal of church growth. It also highlighted another dimension of good boundaries—that boundaries are healthy both for individuals and for the whole congregation!

Since God first called Abraham and Sarah to "go from your country . . . to the land that I will show you" (Genesis 12:1), the people of God have been a people on the move. That God promised to "show" indicates there is a divine plan. Part and parcel of our calling is to prayerfully discern that plan for our lives and personal callings, and through corporate discovery and the hard work of planning in partnership with others, set directions for a faith community as well.

## The Incarnational Church Is a Corporate Body

When asked, "What comes to mind when you hear the word *church*?" seminarians quickly generate a long list with many theological and biblical nouns. Rarely does the word *corporation* appear on the list, however. And yet the apostle Paul's "body language" for the church appears repeatedly in his epistles. As a local manifestation of the body of Christ (*corpus christi* in Latin), in most locales a congregation or other ecclesial organization is a legal corporate entity, a property owner/steward that requires attention to matters of maintenance, insurance, paying bills to retain utility service, and the like.

As a corporate legal entity, a church, like all others, must fulfill certain requirements to remain in good standing. Historical documents, contracts, copies of leases, membership rosters, records of pastoral acts (baptisms, weddings, funerals), which can have legal force in some instances, must be maintained. If anyone is paid for their service to a church, it is an employer bound by many of the same laws as apply to all other employers, including payment of taxes and certain benefits, fair treatment, and safe, harassment-free working conditions. Additionally, while a church or other ecclesial entity is likely to be free from many taxes, as a body it is nevertheless a corporate citizen in a local community and should strive to be of communal service to that locale where God has called it into mission. Many churches make their facilities available free of charge to a wide array of service groups and agencies as part and parcel of fulfilling the mandate voiced by Jeremiah when he exhorted the Israelites to "seek the welfare of the city where I have sent you" (Jer. 29:7), even under conditions of being in foreign exile.

As is the case for all corporate entities, churches must give attention to a wide array of business matters, including personnel supervision and performance reviews, property management, stewarding risk management (insurance), and legal matters (especially during construction projects requiring building permits and the like). Many public ministers are fortunate to serve in congregations replete with a strong cadre of lay leaders who tend to many or most of these administrative matters. Other colleagues, however, soon discover upon arriving in their new calls that a host of such mundane matters have long been ignored. While serving on a regional judicatory staff, Michael was once asked to help a congregation that presented me at our first meeting with a box full of several years' unopened bank statements! Under such circumstances, it can be a challenge to motivate and equip and train or seek training for lay leaders to fulfill many administrative responsibilities. But until such leadership development occurs, at times the minister may have to see to it that the water and electric bills are paid on time, lest one end up sitting in a dark study or find the pipes frozen on a chilly winter morning.

There may be a church somewhere that holds no meetings other than its worship gatherings, but we haven't found one yet! Preparing for, participating in, and leading meetings is on almost every public minister's weekly schedule. While a more extended treatment of "making meetings matter" appears elsewhere,[9] a few brief suggestions are offered here to assist readers in this aspect of ministerial practice. Preparation and advance distribution of an agenda is key, and ideally others involved in leadership (committee chairs or parish officers) can share this responsibility. Receiving an agenda in advance signals to meeting participants that their time will be valued and well spent; it also enables their buy-in if accompanied by a request for additions. An agenda enables the one chairing the meeting to keep discussions on track and moving to decisions. Orientation for those new to a council, committee, or work group is likewise essential. Nothing can be more embarrassing to a newcomer than to have to ask countless questions about routine matters that could have been clarified by providing a few key documents like bylaws, past meeting minutes, and newsletter articles about ongoing programs. Conflict often arises in congregations as a result of basic communication lapses or the lack of record keeping. Not all meetings require formal minute taking, but including brief summaries in bulletins, newsletters, or emails to members about important decisions or new program proposals can go a long way in avoiding frustrations caused when communication is left to the rumor mill and gossip chain.

As corporate legal entities, churches and their leaders must also give attention to such matters as reviewing, revising, and following governing documents like constitutions, bylaws, and various policies. It is surprising how often ministers and congregations unnecessarily get themselves into trouble simply because they ignore their own documents! Prior to accepting a call, a minister should peruse the constitution, policies, and above all, any written documents that are in essence a job description spelling out expectations for one's leadership role.

Maintaining parish records and documents that are likely to have historical value is another dimension of paperwork that so many ministers seem to dislike. But just as professionals in all other contexts must tend to careful record keeping (would you trust a doctor who kept no charts?), so one who ministers must promptly record events like marriages, baptisms, funerals, and other official acts that may have legal as well as ecclesiastical ramifications. Failure to mail a marriage certificate to the courthouse, for example, can result in a couple's wedding not being legally recorded.

While it is often difficult for us to recognize in the day-to-day practice of ministry, we are making history all the time. Today's seemingly insignificant events may be of keen interest to future historians looking back on our time. Accordingly, attention to preserving key documents, anniversary bulletins, and parish newsletters with particularly significant reports on new programs or tragic events in parish life is important but is often overlooked. The challenge of record keeping has become even more complex in the age of electronic communication, when so many documents once preserved on paper are now stored on flash drives, on email servers, or in "the cloud." Fortunately, most denominations offer helpful guidelines on records retention, as do many local or state historical societies and major universities and other institutions. In this area, as others, ministers fortunate enough to have competent volunteers or staff who tend to these matters may not have to expend much effort other than occasionally reviewing others' work. But in many ministry contexts, the minister may also have to engage in a fair amount of hands-on record keeping and other routine administrative tasks.

In another publication, Michael and his coauthor Robert Bacher offer an entire chapter on "Life under Law: Navigating Legal Matters in Ministry."[10] Suffice it here to offer only a few brief comments in this regard. While Christians are to avoid being legalistic in our interpersonal relationships, we live in this world of laws and complex regulatory environments that impinge on many areas of the church's life. It can be a real gift to parishioners when their ministers offer suggestions and reminders of the importance of engaging in financial planning, having a will, and providing for one's loved ones and cherished causes as a final act of stewardship. As corporate entities, churches and other faith communities must give periodic attention to such mundane matters as reviewing insurance coverage to ensure its adequacy and complying with zoning regulations, permit requirements, and other matters whenever a building or major remodeling project is afoot. And sadly, on occasion a church may be involved in a lawsuit if a

---

**Church-State relations are rarely clear-cut:** While some Christians in the U.S. believe there is an absolute separation between church and government, things are rarely so unambiguous. If a fire breaks out in a church building, most parishioners will rush to make a 911 call and plead for help from a fire company, which typically receives tax dollars and thereby is an agent of the state. Similarly, churches and other religious organizations must comply with certain legal requirements in many areas, including fair employment practices. These are important matters that merit careful discussion by parish or church agency leaders.

---

tragedy has occurred involving its property or allegations against members of the staff, for example. Under many of these kinds of circumstances, an attorney may need to be engaged as a faith community navigates murky legal waters.

## Stewardship and Faithful Financial Leadership

Not mentioned in the chapter on preaching was the fact that Jesus talked about money more than almost any other topic! Nevertheless, so many of us preachers find addressing stewardship one of our greatest challenges. To be sure, this is another area where wise ministers recognize that garnering the financial and other resources required for a church to fulfill its mission is the responsibility of the whole people of God in that place. While some ministers tend to over-function in this arena, and thereby rob the laity of their opportunity to experience the joy of leading stewardship emphases, the greater tendency seems to be avoidance on the part of parish clergy and other staff.

Coming to terms with one's views about money and personal giving is a first step for those who would engage with others in emulating Jesus' bold embrace of the reality that we live in a world whose citizens must render unto Caesar, use money well, and not be enticed by loving it so much it becomes the "root of all evil" (1 Tim. 6:10). This is currently an acutely sensitive matter for beginning ministers financially strapped as a result of borrowing for their seminary educations. In many cases, we are eager to give generously and inspire others by our generosity, yet the pressures of sustaining one's personal and family financial stability is a major constraint.

As in all matters treated in this chapter, how one leads in this arena will vary according to the ministry context. Those called to serve among people living in or on the edge of poverty may need to be very creative in seeking financial resources for the ministry from beyond the parish membership. At the same time, many colleagues serving in such contexts are surprised and

---

**The words *tithe* and *tithing* may be too limiting:** Our English word *steward* has a rich and earthy history, being derived from Old English "sty-ward (*stigweard*)" meaning the keeper of the pig sty or hall! Biblical stewardship is based in deep convictions that *all* we have is a gift from God, and we are accountable to God for our use of the entirety of our money and possessions, as well as our relationships and vocations. In this recognition, exclusive focus on tithing or giving 10 percent of one's income to the church can convey the false impression that an individual is free to do whatever s/he chooses with the other 90 percent.

---

inspired by the self-sacrificial level of giving from those who have little by way of financial resources. It may be even more challenging for colleagues serving among the well-off to encourage generosity and even prophetically question an overreliance upon material wealth. Regardless of context, one should not deny those served the opportunity to respond to God's invitation to be generous stewards. This typically involves joining others in conducting periodic stewardship campaigns, and preaching or teaching about the wise use of money and other resources.

Speaking of the wise use of money leads to making the connection between asking and receiving, as well as to keeping track of income and expenses, and spending prudently and with high accountability. An old adage asks, "When is a business executive not at his or her best?" The answer: "When she or he's in church!" There is a pervasive, probably unconscious split in many folks' thinking that money is dirty (recalling the King James Bible's translation "filthy lucre" [1 Tim. 3:3]) and therefore is not proper to dwell on with any seriousness in the spiritual realm of church. Even in congregations populated with competent financial managers, there is frequently a somewhat lackadaisical attitude with regard to such matters as separation of duties, regular audits, and transparency in fiscal reporting. It is not normally the minister's role to serve as chief financial officer, but in some contexts, part and parcel of public ministry may involve raising questions and offering suggestions based upon denominational guidelines and best practices observed elsewhere. This is not to say we should adopt a prosperity-gospel mode of preaching that loving God will magically equate to amassing riches! But preaching and offering education on a healthy spirituality of money can help overcome people's squeamishness about making hard, practical financial decisions.[11]

## A Given for Today's Ministers: Coping with Conflict

Even in lean economic times, conflict is a growth industry! Nowhere is this more the case than in churches and other faith communities. Once again, we have addressed this topic elsewhere in considerable depth and will not repeat here much of which can be gleaned from many outstanding experts' work related to conflict.[12] But avoiding the topic altogether would be failing to share with readers the full scope of ministerial leadership in our time.

While a survey of personality types reflected among those who pursue public ministry as a vocation suggests we are even more conflict-averse than the average person, no other professionals in society are as likely to have to deal with it on a regular basis than the clergy. Faith communities are highly charged arenas in which emotions run high, precisely because churches are dedicated to higher things. When disagreements arise, they often escalate rapidly because persons involved are convinced that their perspectives are God-given or that something deeply sacred to them is at stake. Unlike most other locales beyond the home (school, workplace, recreational facilities, etc.), church is also a place to which many come as families. Often the tensions and conflict that exist within families get writ large in congregations, and the colliding conflicts of multiple families can generate a chaotic scene for the entire community, which also functions as a parallel "family system."[13]

In the brief treatment that can be included here, we offer a mere beginning guide to coping with conflict. Seminarians or new ministers will do well to seek out seminars and workshops on conflict; increasingly these are offered by denominations, community colleges, and other professional continuing-education providers. A first principle to embrace is simply this: hang in there! You'll likely survive your first and many subsequent parish conflicts, though it won't be easy. Support from a trusted colleague, mentor, or pastoral counselor can be extremely helpful for gaining perspective. Becoming a student of the conflict—that is, trying to understand the background, multiple interwoven relational patterns, and the surface and deeper issues involved—can enable one to take a step back and perhaps avoid taking things personally. Studying historical trends in a parish or organization may reveal some interesting patterns and underlying values that lead to conflict. For example, in consulting with a California parish undergoing severe conflict, Michael discovered that this congregation tended to endure a major upheaval about every five years. Further detective work revealed how much the members valued forgiveness—and to forgive and be forgiven, you have to be fighting with somebody! While no one would concede it at first, this congregation's modus operandi seemed to simply require that the members periodically find things about which to fight in order that they could then go on to forgive one another and move forward.

Conflicts may also be symbolic of deeper fissures in the congregation that were caused by an earlier (sometimes much earlier) trauma to the whole congregational system. Church consultant Nancy Myers Hopkins describes a heated conflict in one congregation over whether to replace an old altar rail with a new one or remove it altogether. Logical arguments for and against seemed unable to move the congregation toward any negotiated solution. With the consultant's help, the congregation finally came to realize that the real conflict was over a long-sealed-over trauma of clergy sexual misconduct in the congregation. The altar rail had come to express and at the same time safely disguise the real conflict, which was too painful to talk about: whether or not the new pastor could be trusted or should be fenced off from the flock![14]

Earlier in the chapter, we made the case for continual planning as a key to organizational health and forward movement. At this juncture, it needs to be acknowledged that almost any effective planning process will itself generate conflict, since not all members or participants will agree on directions that emerge as future goals. Simply being prepared for this inevitable result of planning can help keep leaders from freaking out when conflict comes as change begins to occur and plans are formulated and implemented.

To conclude this short introductory segment on conflict, we again underscore the value and importance of collegiality and a consultative style of ministry. It can be invaluable to seek support from others and receive some objective feedback and critique from peers or a professional counselor not directly involved in a conflict. Self-examination and the willingness to reconsider one's own interactions are important as well. While we ministers should never take too many things personally, neither can we afford to become jaded or cynical to the point we cannot acknowledge that, when conflicts arise, sometimes we are part of the problem!

## Leading in the World beyond the Congregation or Other Organization

For many of us, John Wesley's testimony that "I look upon all the world as my parish"[15] continues to ring true more than two centuries after he uttered these famous words. Public ministers, in other words, often have opportunities to be leaders in multiple arenas beyond the congregations, organizations, or institutions where we spend most of our time and from which we draw our salaries. Some who venture into being public servants may hold elected office—as local village or city officials, or even in larger circles as state or federal legislators. Most ministers will serve in less visible and demanding capacities as board members in civic organizations or local governmental entities and as ethics advisers or volunteer chaplains in hospitals, fire companies, police departments, and the like. Still others exercise a portion of their ministry through compensated board membership with banks or businesses. In the case of these paid positions, it is probably important to have clear understandings as to whether the income received is retained personally or shared wholly or in part with the primary employing congregation or other organization.

Beyond such service in elected positions or volunteer leadership, a minister's public witness may be exercised through writing and speaking to audiences beyond the congregation. The minister might compose opinion pieces or letters to the editor, a personal or ministry blog, sermons or addresses for broadcast, and other publishing or speaking activity intended for broad audiences. When a minister is involved in such public theologizing, it can be important to distinguish when one is speaking personally versus being an official spokesperson for a church or other ministry. This becomes particularly critical in matters related to political campaigns and possible endorsement of partisan candidates for elected office. A lack of care in this regard can compromise a church's nonprofit tax status. If in doubt in these kinds of matters, seek advice from denominational officials or other advisers conversant in the nuances of church-state relations.

## The Kind of Leaders Needed for Tomorrow's Church

We are keenly aware of the fermentation bubbling up almost everywhere today surrounding the kind of leaders needed currently and in the future if the church is to not merely survive but thrive in the postmodern context of the twenty-first century.[16] We tend to resist what we regard as some overstatement of how much the church has changed in the past several decades, thereby requiring a totally new kind of leader. To be sure, significant changes have occurred, yet prior generations of leaders have encountered their own huge challenges and the need to adapt amidst swirling changes. In the commencement address at Gettysburg Seminary, Michael offered some comparisons of our time to the events of 1864, 1914, and 1964. Those were all tumultuous times when many were arguing that the church and its leaders would have to look different and act dramatically differently than before. Notwithstanding our tendency to be a bit more cautious than many in calling for drastic change, we do share the conviction that ministry requires new skills, attitudes, and relational abilities not required when we were first ordained. However, no time in the church's history has been easy; we can take some reassurance in the midst of challenges by realizing that those who have gone before us also struggled to manage problems, transitions, and traumas in their own day, and the church has survived!

Many of those who speak and write about the kinds of church leaders needed in today's and tomorrow's world orbit around a few key words like *transformational, missional, entrepreneurial, adaptable, ecumenical* (and increasingly *interfaith* in perspective), and comfortable in the *pluralistic global community*. The current tagline of Columbia Theological Seminary is "educating *imaginative, resilient* leaders for God's changing world." These descriptors all point to and emanate from conclusions that there are few if any ministry settings where a business-as-usual or "keep doing it as we always have" stance will result in stable let alone vibrant and growing faith communities. Gone are the days when a pastor, priest, or other minister could accept a call to a stable congregation and simply tend faithfully to the

---

**Where do I find my "job description"?** While some churches craft formal written position descriptions for all employees, including clergy, in many cases a pastor or priest may need to go in search of other documents that spell out broad expectations for the work they are called to do. In many denominations the governing documents (constitution and bylaws) contain a section on "Ministry" or "The Clergy," which cite a long list of duties and responsibilities. Periodic review of these expectations, in dialogue with key parish leaders, can serve as the basis for promoting mutual understanding and avoiding unnecessary conflicts over "what the pastor should be doing."

---

existing members. More and more, the church has to compete for people's time, energy, loyalty, and commitment with a growing number of attractive leisure and recreational pursuits as well as their demanding jobs and otherwise overfilled personal and family lives. And while it may be overstated by some alarmist authors and speakers, there is no doubt that our society has experienced a decline in religious interest or at least willingness to actively engage in and support institutionalized forms of religious expression like congregations. So indeed, adaptability, creativity, a certain entrepreneurial spirit, and willingness to take risks, meet new people, and invite them into a faith community are requirements for church leaders, perhaps to a much higher degree than in some previous generations.

And where and how might one become equipped for such leadership in the church of today and tomorrow? Seminaries often become the targets for those convinced there is no such place in which new types of leadership are being inculcated in students eager to become transformational leaders who will flourish amidst all these challenging circumstances. In a critique of his seminary, one frustrated cleric blurted out to its president, "Stop preparing leaders for a church that no longer exists!"[17]

While we believe that seminaries and divinity schools are on occasion unfairly and excessively criticized (especially the ones where we serve!), we do agree that many of the areas addressed in this chapter, which are required to practice effectively the art of ministry in today's challenging contexts, do not receive adequate attention in many curricula. Most seminaries offer at best one course in church administration, and in few if any is it a required course. While themes related to creative and adaptive leadership may be touched upon in biblical studies or theology and church history courses, the kind of readings and discussions common in business, law, or even medical schools on such practical matters tend to be more absent in seminaries and divinity schools. Given the perennial debate whether such an elusive topic as leadership can be taught at all (versus being an innate talent given to some individuals and not to others), it is not likely that there will be dramatic changes in this reality anytime soon. Accordingly, persons preparing for ecclesiastical leadership roles may need to turn to resources outside the seminary, reading widely in literature found in the business section of a bookstore or online catalog. Another means by which a minister-in-formation can grow in her or his own capacity to be an effective leader and competent administrator is by observing, interviewing, and hanging around with clerics and other ministers regarded by peers as highly competent and effective. By whatever means, we are convinced, the gifts and graces required for servant leadership can be acquired, and they must continually be renewed and upgraded in order for ministers to serve faithfully in the places where we are called to stay and break bread together.

**Questions for Personal Exploration**

1. Jesus often taught in parables, conveying a spiritual insight by comparison to something concrete. Complete the following thought: A servant leader in a community of faith is like _____.
2. Thinking about leaders you have known (including perhaps yourself), who has been more authoritative, and who more authoritarian? What were these leaders' respective impacts on their organizations or communities?
3. Have you been involved in a serious conflict in your congregation or another organization? What role did you play? How was the conflict resolved (if it was)?
4. What feelings come up for you around the word *money*? How do you feel about the prospect of asking for money in order to support the mission of the church? How comfortable are you in assuming some role in stewarding a church's resources? Would you characterize your own attitude toward money more as one of frugality and scarcity or as one of abundance?
5. This chapter discusses how planning is always discerning God's call to mission and also requires strategic and practical steps. What call are you discerning from God in your life today, and what practical steps do you need to take to follow that calling?

 **Resources for Deeper Exploration**

Bacher, Robert, and Michael Cooper-White. *Church Administration: Programs, Process, Purpose.* Minneapolis: Fortress Press, 2007.

Becker, Carol E. *Becoming Colleagues: Women and Men Serving Together in Faith.* San Francisco: Jossey-Bass, 2000.

Crumroy, Otto F. Jr., Stan Kukawka, and Frank M. Witman. *Church Administration and Finance Manual: Resources for Leading the Local Church.* New York: Morehouse, 1998.

Everist, Norma Cook, and Craig L. Nessan. *Transforming Leadership: New Vision for a Church in Mission.* Minneapolis: Fortress Press, 2008.

Heifetz, Ronald A., and Marty Linsky. *Leadership on the Line: Staying Alive through the Dangers of Leading.* Cambridge, MA: Harvard Business Review Press, 2002.

## 👓 Notes

1. One of those who uses the term is Robert K. Greenleaf, whose *Servant Leadership: A Journey into the Nature of Legitimate Power and Greatness* (New York: Paulist Press, 1991) remains an enduring classic in leadership studies.

2. Margaret Wheatley, *Leadership and the New Science: Discovering Order in a Chaotic World*, 2nd ed. (San Francisco: Berrett-Koehler, 2001).

3. Edwin Friedman, *Generation to Generation: Family Process in Church and Synagogue* (New York: Guilford, 1985, 2011), 3 et passim.

4. For more on this issue, see Pamela Cooper-White, *The Cry of Tamar: Violence against Women and the Church's Response*, 2nd ed. (Minneapolis: Fortress Press, 2012), 149–67.

5. For example, Robert Bacher and Michael Cooper-White, "When Conflict Comes Calling," ch. 11 in *Church Administration: Programs, Process, Purpose* (Minneapolis: Fortress Press, 2007).

6. National organizations include Gamaliel, PICO (originally Pacific Institute for Community Organizations; now PICO National Network), the Industrial Areas Foundation (IAF), and others. For good introductions to faith-based community organizing, see PICO National Network, "What Is Faith-Based Community Organizing?," http://www.piconetwork.org/about/faith-based-community-organizing; Peter Heitzel and Alexia Salvatierra, *Faith-Rooted Organizing: Mobilizing the Church in Service to the World* (Downers Grove, IL: InterVarsity, 2013).

7. John P. Kretzmann and John L. McKnight, *Building Communities from the Inside Out: A Path toward Finding and Mobilizing a Community's Assets* (Chicago: ACTA, 1993). See the website of the Asset Based Community Development Institute, School of Education and Social Policy, Northwestern University, http://www.abcdinstitute.org/. See also Luther K. Snow, *The Power of Asset Mapping: How Your Congregation Can Act on Its Gifts* (Washington, DC: Alban Institute, 2004).

8. The shepherd/rancher dichotomy is widely used by many authors and church consultants. See, for example, C. Peter Wagner, *Church Planting for a Greater Harvest: A Comprehensive Guide* (Eugene, OR: Wipf & Stock, 2010), 134; Lyle Schaller, *Survival Tactics in the Parish* (Nashville: Abingdon, 1977), 52.

9. Bacher and Cooper-White, *Church Administration*, 165 ff.

10. Ibid., 265 ff.

11. For more on this concept and resources for implementation, see the website of the Faith and Money Network, www.faithandmoneynetwork.org.

12. See especially various publications by Speed Leas, Peter Steinke, and Hugh Halverstadt.

13. Edwin Friedman, *From Generation to Generation: Family Process in Church and Synagogue* (New York: Guilford, 1985).

14. Nancy Myers Hopkins, "Symbolic Church Fights: The Hidden Agenda When Clerical Trust Has Been Betrayed," *Congregation: The Alban Journal* (May/June 1993): 15–18.

15. John Wesley, "All the World My Parish," in *The Journal of John Wesley*, ch. 3, written 1789, Christian Classics Ethereal Library, http://www.ccel.org/ccel/wesley/journal .vi.iii.v.html.

16. Both authors have offered succinct summaries of postmodernism in other publications. See Pamela Cooper-White, *Shared Wisdom: The Use of the Self in Pastoral Care and Counseling* (Minneapolis: Fortress Press, 2004), 36–43; and Michael Cooper-White, *The Comeback God: A Theological Primer for a Life of Faith* (Minneapolis: Augsburg, 2009), 31–38.

17. David Tiede, president emeritus of Luther Seminary in St. Paul, Minnesota, recounted this statement on many occasions. It was made to him early during his presidency as he sought advice from many groups and individuals.

## Epilogue

# Journey into Joy

> Then they told what had happened on the road, and how he had
> been made known to them in the breaking of the bread.
>
> —Luke 24:35

L ate in the day of that first Easter, two anonymous travelers headed homeward toward their village named Emmaus. We can imagine they had already begun to put behind them all the hopes they had held for the dashing young prophet named Jesus who was "mighty in deed and word before God and all the people" (Luke 24:19). As occurs after the death of a loved one, they were reminiscing about the good times even as they relived the anguish of his horrific death. But the overwhelming mood was one of loss, despair, and the prospect of a bleak future devoid of hope.

Then they encountered the stranger who "came near and went with them" (v. 15). Although they did not recognize him, there was something about him that enabled them to open their hearts and spill their guts. "We had hoped that he was the one to redeem Israel," they lamented (v. 21). "But now all has come to naught; he is dead and we shall know no redemption for ourselves or our people."

Later at table, as bread was broken after they had issued their call for the stranger to remain in ministry among them, "their eyes were opened and they recognized him" (v. 31). Then he vanished into the new future that they had so long awaited and that he had consistently promised. So they could no longer remain comfortable in their homes and village. Back to Jerusalem! On the road again, but now with a mission, they accepted their own callings. One more time they would see him. This time it was their turn to offer him his final meal, "a piece of broiled fish" (vv. 36 ff.). And then he led them out on the road again, this time to Bethany, "and lifting up his hands he blessed them. While he blessed them, he parted from then and was carried up into heaven. And they returned to Jerusalem with great joy, and were continually in the temple blessing God" (vv. 50-53).

In this short book, we have endeavored to invite our readers into a conversation as we shared a journey contemplating some of the practices of ministry as we understand our calling in this time. We hope that in some small measure our reflections have conveyed to our readers a broader understanding of the calling for which you are preparing or in which you may already be engaged. We are serious about this being a *conversation* and a shared journey, hoping for opportunities in the days and years ahead to meet some of you in person. We also covet your reflections in writing as you may be moved to share them with us.[1]

From our own experiences and those of many colleagues, we are aware that a book such as this runs the risk of rendering the practice of ministry an occupation that can be mastered like any other by means of working hard, garnering and honing a skill set, and pleasing the "customers" who come shopping for the spiritual wares we peddle. May it not be so! As signaled in the introduction, the book offers no well-tested recipes guaranteed to produce "success" in public ministry, whatever form it may take. If we have offered encouragement for the journey, together with some imperfect but hopefully helpful road maps, we are grateful. In the end, we confess some uneasiness with the assigned topic, for the very terminology *practices of ministry* can imply that a journey of faith can be reduced to a set of tasks or performances. True ministry in the Spirit of the One who walked the Emmaus way with the dejected disciples flows ultimately from neither our tasks nor our performances, but only and always from God's loving promises.

It is in the love and the promises of God, summed up by the risen Christ in another gospel proclamation, "Behold, I am with you always, to the close of the age" (Matt. 28:20), that we encounter the essence of our callings. As we cling to that love and that promise, we enter into joy.

We end on a note of personal reflection, even testimony. Like many of the schools accredited by the Association of Theological Schools (ATS) in the United States and Canada, the seminaries where we serve offer our seniors every year the opportunity to complete the ATS Graduating Student Questionnaire.[3] By means of this tool, those about to complete their seminary sojourns can offer feedback on their experiences in a broad array of areas—for example, their classroom experience, professors' availability outside of class, and even the quality of the school's student housing and refectory or dining hall food. The final question each year requires a simple yes-or-no answer to indicate agreement or disagreement with the following sentence: "If I had it to do over, I would come here again."

Following several decades of engagement in this calling, each of us— your companions on this journey of reflection on the practices, potential pitfalls, and promises of ministry—answer with a resounding "Yes! If we had it to do over, we would come this way again!" We have found joy. Not just momentary happiness or satisfaction, although those have been there for us, too, but the deep joy that wells up from authentically sharing life, with all its ups and downs, with others in the body of Christ. In our ministries, we have been immersed in hilarity and tragedy, exhilaration and drudgery, calm and anxiety, empathy and pettiness, peacefulness and anger, life and death. We have succeeded and failed at times to maintain the "nonanxious presence" that is recommended for pastoral leadership.[4] Through it all, we have found strength and consolation in the knowledge that the risen Christ has been walking the way with us, even when we did not recognize him. Further, he will be there at journey's end and has already prepared for us—as he has for everyone—a feast, a most holy feast.

## ◉◉ Notes

1. The authors' contact information is available on their respective seminary websites: Pamela at Columbia Theological Seminary (http://www.ctsnet.edu/faculty-member?id=9) and Michael at the Lutheran Theological Seminary at Gettysburg (http://www.ltsg.edu).

2. For more information about the Association of Theological Schools' Student Data Services, see ATS, "Student Data," http://www.ats.edu/resources/student-data, accessed August 21, 2014.

3. Edwin Friedman, *Generation to Generation: Family Process in Church and Synagogue* (New York: Guilford, 1985, 2011), 3 et passim.